THE HISTORY & LOCAL POST

OF

RATTLESNAKE ISLAND LAKE ERIE

by

John Wells

THE HISTORY & LOCAL POST OF RATTLESNAKE ISLAND, LAKE ERIE

Copyright © John Wells 2003

ISBN: 1 903607 41 8

All rights reserved. No part of this publication may be reproduced, stored in a retrieval system or transmitted in any form or by any means electronic, mechanical, photocopying or otherwise without the prior permission in writing of the copyright holder.

Typeset and Published by:

Able Publishing
13 Station Road
Knebworth
Hertfordshire
SG3 6AP

Tel: (01438) 814316 / 812320   Fax: (01438) 815232
Web: www.ablepublishing.co.uk
Email: fp@ablepublishing.co.uk

Dedication

*To my dear devoted wife Marion
for her patience, tolerance and understanding.*

*To my son and daughter, David and Michelle,
who have worked so hard to achieve successful
careers during difficult times.*

*Also to my dear sister Frances and husband Alf,
who reside a short distance from the Great Lakes.*

*Lastly to Gladys who has kept me
sustained with refreshments each day.*

James P. Frackelton MD
Founder of Rattlesnake Island Stamps

CONTENTS

          page

i. Acknowledgements 6

ii. Introduction 8

1. The Early Inhabitants 11

2. The Lake Erie Islands 16

3. The Erie Islands Postal Service 20

4. The Erie Islands Aircraft (The Tin Goose) 32

5. Rattlesnake Island Local Airmail Post 44

6. Postal Administration People 58

7. Catalogue of Stamp Issues 66

8. Rattlesnake Island Local Post Cancellations 98

9. Rattlesnake Island Ford Tri-motor Markings 99

10. Rattlesnake Island Local Post Inscriptions 100

11. Known U.S. Post Office Cancellations on RI LP Covers 102

12. A Selection of Stamp Errors - Genuine or ...? 103

ACKNOWLEDGEMENTS

From the inception of the Rattlesnake Island local airmail post in 1966, these unique stamps aroused considerable interest among collectors from all over the world. Despite the fact that no stamps have been issued since 1989, interest continues to grow, thus the stamps, covers and memorabilia are much sought after. During the period that the island's stamps were issued, several people began to compile lists of the issues, or penned short articles about them. Over recent years, as a result of my curiosity and in response to enquiries, many of those same people have very generously sent copies of articles, newspaper cuttings, photographs and other detail. My researches however, revealed that no truly up to date listing or colour illustrated catalogue of all the stamp issues exists, nor any comprehensive historical record. Thus since I have long cherished the desire to write, but have never really felt confident enough to put pen to paper, this particular subject intrigued me so much that I felt an overwhelming desire to have a go.

I have therefore attempted to create a useful historic reference for the benefit of collectors by collating all the information so kindly contributed, together with my own internet research and the enthusiastic support and encouragement of fellow collectors across the "pond", who, as yet, I have not had the pleasure of meeting, (hopefully that pleasure will come in the near future) but nevertheless regard them as very good friends.

Firstly, I must express my sincere and grateful thanks to lifetime collector and exhibitor of postal history, Bob Fritz who has provided me with so much information. Also, James P Frackelton M.D. the founder and designer of the Rattlesnake Island stamps, and who set the record straight where uncertainty of the facts existed, thus ensuring a true account of events. Without their valuable help this book would not have been possible.

My thanks also go to the following people who contributed

items of interest, those who very kindly gave their permission to include extracts from their work, or to re-produce catalogue listings pertaining to the Rattlesnake Island stamps and covers, various organisations who published articles now resting in their archives; my grateful thanks go to Jack C. Standen, William R. Schultz, Howard R. Lutz, Christer Brunstrom, Ralph Nafziger, Barry Newton, The American First Day Cover Society - extracts re-printed with the kind permission of the author and editor, for more information contact the Society at www.AFDCS.org, Ray Dauterman, David Turnbull, Dale L. Liebenthal, Fred L. Hoffman, P. Tubach, James Dysarczyk, Gerald A. Estes, Jacob Kisner, Johnson Klosinski, Jay Eaker, Tom Root (Aerial Photos), John E. Rees, (Ford Tri-Motor Photos), Linn's Stamp News, 'The Blade' Toledo, Ohio, Ford Archives, 'The Plain Dealer', Ohio Geological Survey, Center For Archival Collections, National Air and Space Museum, Smithsonian Institution, Ohio Historical Society, Eric G. Swedin - 'The Battle of Lake Erie', E.S. Curtis - 'The North American Indian', United States Post Office.

Whilst every effort is made to seek the permission of all copyright owners to reproduce items in full or part, or for research and reference purposes, in endeavouring to ensure that all contributions are duly acknowledged, there is always the danger of causing offence or contravention of the rules by ommission. I therefore wish to make it clear that any failure on my part to acknowledge a contributor, and who may feel aggrieved, is entirely unintentional and an oversight on my part for which I truly regret and apologise.

Sincerely, John Wells.

INTRODUCTION

My first encounter with Rattlesnake Island, previously completely unknown to me, was back in 1999, or thereabouts, when a collector specialising in stamps depicting lighthouses, sent me a paper cutting which illustrated a set of three lighthouse stamps from Rattlesnake Island, and could I try to obtain them for his collection. In fact several other requests for these stamps subsequently arrived, presumably as news of their existence spread among collectors. As a result of this seemingly sudden interest in these stamps, curiosity got the better of me and I began to make enquiries about this island and its post. The more I investigated, the more intrigued I became, and as my research discovered that the local postage stamps were produced for only a relatively short period and discontinued after 1989, it seemed clear to me there was a need to place on record, as much information as possible for posterity, hence this book. Perhaps I should add that although I began collecting the stamps a short time later, the lighthouse stamps for the collectors, or myself, still remain elusive, so these along with several other issues continue to be a challenge.

Rattlesnake Island lies in the American waters of Lake Erie. For many people, particularly those who live in urban areas, or relatively small country communities of the world, or who may rarely travel beyond their own locality, their vision of a lake is probably little more than an extra large pond.

To actually see for one's self, fine examples of such enormous expanses of inland water, in fact the largest fresh water inland sea in the world, one needs to travel to the Great Lakes of North America. These were created during the Ice Age when nature's might and power forced an ice mass to carve its way northward through the American state of Ohio, gouging massive grooves into the earth's surface. Glaciers of tremendous weight and power left deep depressions in the earth, which subsequently filled when the ice melted. Today commercial shipping lines sail from the

Atlantic ocean up the St Lawrence river and on through the man-made St Lawrence Seaway, which divides Canada from the United States of America, past the Thousand Islands district and on into the first of the five Great Lakes, Lake Ontario, one of the smaller lakes, although this in itself is of a considerable size, and proudly reflects the majesty of Toronto's skyline. To the southwest of Lake Ontario lies Lake Erie, whilst to the north and west the much larger lakes of Huron, Michigan and Superior spread over literally so many hundreds of miles, one might be mistaken into thinking they were truly looking out to sea.

Generally, one would imagine the waters of a lake to be ever calm and tranquil, but the natural make-up of Lake Erie, whose waters surround a number of islands, is an integral and essential feature leading to the main theme of this book. The aftermath of the ice age activity, does in fact mean that its waters are relatively shallow in geological terms, thus it is subject to quite violent storms and high waves, perhaps whilst witnessing such an event, it is yet another reason for one to feel convinced they are on a sea coast, and not a lake.

Having now formed a mental picture of great waterways thousands of miles from any sea or ocean, it is probably equally breathtaking to realise that within the boundaries of Lake Erie for instance, several islands of varying sizes exist. This of course, also applies to many other lakes, but the purpose of this book is to offer the reader and collector a little insight into the events and early habitation, eventually leading up to the postal history of one particularly notable tract of land bearing the somewhat sinister name of Rattlesnake Island, and the associated neighbouring islands linked to mainland districts on which it depends. The islands we see today were also formed from the after effects of the powerful forces of ice movement. Some of the larger islands in the lake are permanently inhabited and commercially used today. Also, despite its location which can subject it to very severe winters, Lake Erie has high nutrient levels and relatively warm temperatures thus encouraging a greater abundance of fish varieties, and of course, offers excellent fishing during both summer and winter.

Perhaps more than the other lakes, Erie's history is fascinating and particularly notable for its involvement in historic battles, in particular, the war of 1812, but even before the recorded conflicts between the British and Americans at that time, the islands of Lake Erie were part of the historic Firelands Section of the Connecticut Land Company's Western Reserve.

The Connecticut Western Reserve Lands, claimed under an English Charter in 1662 by King Charles II, covered approximately 3.3 million acres taking in 14 northeastern Ohio counties starting at the Pennsylvania - Ohio line and extending 120 miles westward to the present Seneca and Sandusky County lines. Bounded in the north by Lake Erie, and in the south by the parallel of the 41st degree north latitude, running just south of the present day cities of Youngstown, Akron and Willard.

1. The Early Inhabitants

Going back to the late 1500s, the area bordering Lake Erie's southern coastline was occupied by the Erie Indians who gave their name to the lake, and were said to number around 15,000. Their territory stretched from Northern Ohio nearly to Buffalo, New York. It also took in Kelleys Island and probably most of the other islands in Lake Erie. However, by about 1635, the Erie Indians were being forced eastward and inland from Lake Erie by the fierce Iroquois Indians. By 1650, the Erie Indian territory had diminished to an area east of the Cuyahoga River. From 1635 to 1657, the two Indian tribes were locked in a war in which the ferocious Iroquois Indians annihilated the Erie tribe. The Iroquois Indians were in fact, supplied with muskets and other supplies by the Dutch and English settlers, and later on, by the French. At the end of the war, it is reckoned that only 500 to 600 Erie Indians survived, these were mostly women and children that, it is thought, were subsequently absorbed into the Iroquois tribes, although there are other views that some merged with the Seneca tribe in Oklahoma.

In the years that followed the virtual demise of the Erie Indians, and prior to the War of 1812, the Lake Erie islands were occupied by Ottawa and Huron (Wyandot) tribes. It is believed that the Ottawa tribe actually gave Rattlesnake Island its name. The original domain of the Huron tribe was east of Lake Huron in Canada. In 1648, after a series of conflicts with the Iroquois, they became involved in a final battle resulting in their complete demoralization. A large number were either killed or kept in captivity among several Iroquois tribes, or died from hunger and exposure in their struggle to escape to freedom. Some found sanctuary amongst other tribes, but wherever they fled they were pursued by the vengeful Iroquois. Eventually, by a treaty made in1666 between the French and the Iroquois, the Hurons were allowed to move to Michilimackinac, Michigan, and later became established at Sandusky, Ohio. Despite being greatly depleted in numbers, during that time, they attained considerable influence among the tribes of the Great Lakes and the Ohio river.

During the French and Indian wars, the Hurons sided with the French and entered Pontiac's War of 1763 - 66 in an effort to remove the British from the Great Lakes. Following the War of 1812, in 1815 a large reservation was set aside for them in northwestern Ohio and southeastern Michigan, but four years later a part of this land was sold and the remainder was disposed of in 1842 when the Hurons moved to a large reservation in Wyandotte County, Kansas. By treaty of 1855 the Hurons became citizens and in 1867 tribal relations were re-established and they moved to northeastern Indian Territory, Oklahoma.

Proof of Indian occupation of the islands can be found on Kelleys Island where carvings and pictographic writings over 500 years old, are etched in the massive limestone boulder known as Inscription Rock. All the Indian tribes, including the Ottawa, were eventually moved out by European settlers.

The group of islands in Lake Erie situated just north of the southern coastline, including Rattlesnake Island, were part of the "Fire Lands" (also known as Sufferers Lands) within the state of Connecticut's Western Land Reserve. This area consisted of approximately 5,260 square miles of land. Under the Royal Charter by King Charles II in 1662, Connecticut's boundaries were established as extending "from sea to sea" across North America, although royal grants had also created New York and Pennsylvania, both of which encroached on Connecticut's lands.

In September 1781, the British invaded Connecticut. They destroyed by fire the towns of New London, Greenville, Fairfield, Danbury, Ridgefield, Norwalk, New and East Haven and Groton. More than 1,800 supporters of the American Revolution suffered because of the destruction of the nine towns. It was these areas that became known as the Fire Lands. In 1792, Connecticut set aside half a million acres at the west end of the Reserve to compensate these people.

Having ceded all her western lands claims, except the Reserve, to the United States government in 1786, on September 2nd 1795, the state of Connecticut sold the Western Reserve, except the Fire

Lands, to the Connecticut Land Company which consisted of 48 individuals who pledged money to acquire the land. In 1796 the Connecticut Land Company decided to subdivide their purchase into five-mile-square surveying townships. Following this period the Sufferers meantime, their heirs or legal representatives, formed an Ohio Corporation in 1803 to manage their Ohio lands. By 1808 they too had divided their land into five-mile-square surveying townships, but further subdivided these into four-quarter townships containing 4,000 acres each, by so doing they now had 120 equal parts and they then proceeded to draw lots to determine which plot of land each individual would receive. During the course of these transactions Rattlesnake Island was bought by Alfred Pierpont Edwards in 1807.

The islands are basically composed of limestone bedrock but with rich top soil, thus encouraging the growth of red cedars and lush vegetation, whilst underground, as on Kelleys Island in particular, caverns are to be found. The islands and shoreline support a variety of reptiles, including a high concentration of harmless fox snake. At one time the islands were home to the timber rattlesnake, they were in abundance on Rattlesnake Island, hence its name, although it is doubtful the island was so infested that for anyone stepping ashore they would encounter several snakes with every step taken, as was the general belief. In any case, any that may have existed have long since left the area. There are however, conflicting views on how Rattlesnake Island acquired its name, some say that the Ottawa Indians were responsible because they thought the shape of the island with its two dot islands at the western tip forming the rattles, and with the other end rising out of the water, this gave the appearance of a rattlesnake basking in the sun.

The war of 1812 saw the end of the Indian tribes around the islands, and with it, the elimination of further threats by them upon the European settlers in Ohio. Between August 16th and September 27th 1813, Oliver Hazard Perry used the island of South Bass and its harbour, (originally called "Pudding Bay" as shown on a chart drawn in 1789, and later referred to as "Puden Bay" taken from the log of a British ship), now named Put In Bay, as

*Figure 1.
Oliver Hazard Perry*

his base of operations against the British. It was after the successful defeat of the British on September 10th 1813, that Perry wrote the famous and now well documented report of victory, **"We have met the enemy and they are ours......"**

Perry was born on August 23rd 1785, at South Kingston, Rhode Island, of Quaker parentage. His father was in the United States Navy, and at the tender age of 13, Perry also entered naval service as a midshipman aboard the "General Greene", under his father's command. In 1805, at the age of 20, Perry became a Lieutenant and was given command of a small schooner. His skills were quickly recognised and he was called to supervise the construction of several gunboats ordered by President Thomas Jefferson. On completion of this work, Perry was given the command of the 14 gun ship, Revenge. Unfortunately, whilst patrolling the waters of Eastern United States in bad weather, his ship was wrecked on a reef. Following an enquiry, Perry was completely exonerated from any blame and in May 1812 Perry returned to active duty on promotion. A month later the United States declared war on Great Britain, and after being posted to Sacket's Harbour in Lake Ontario, Perry was sent to supervise the construction of six vessels at Lake Erie, which was completed by July 1813.

The Battle of Lake Erie began with Perry aboard his flagship Lawrence which was severely damaged with the loss of many lives through the constant pounding from British gunfire. Perry transferred and took command of the war ship Niagara and sailed her into battle, firing broadsides at the British who had already suffered heavy losses. This action actually forced their surrender within 15 minutes of Perry's transfer, thus followed those now legendary words. After his victory, Perry was again promoted, to the rank of Captain and was subsequently sent to Venezuela on a diplomatic mission, after which alas, he contracted yellow fever and died at sea near Trinidad on August 23rd 1819, his 34th birthday. In 1826 his remains were moved to Newport, Rhode Island where a monument in his honour was erected by the state. A curious fact remains that despite several United States postage stamps depicting the head of Perry in profile have been issued, (see Figures 2 and 3) to date, not one has ever been produced to commemorate the Battle of Lake Erie or the Perry Memorial.

Figure 2   *Figure 3*

Perry's victory gave the Americans control of Lake Erie and a period of relative calm prevailed amongst the islands. In 1854 Joseph de Rivera San Jargo purchased six of the islands, South Bass, Middle Bass, Sugar, Gibraltar, Ballast and Starve. He turned Put In Bay into a sheep farm with a flock of over 2,000 animals. He later discontinued with the sheep and converted the island into a fruit farm. On August 22nd of the same year Abigail Dunning of Hartford, Connecticut sold North Bass Island and Rattlesnake Island to Horace Kelly of Cleveland, Ohio. On June 22nd 1861 Rattlesnake Island became part of Put In Bay Township. In the early 1900s a family by the name of Hammond lived on the island. A further notable event concerns the 225 foot sidewheel steamer 'State of Ohio' which on the 20th September 1906 tried to run over the island in thick fog and was grounded until October 17th when two tugs finally pulled her afloat.

2. The Lake Erie Islands

To enable the reader to further envisage the sheer magnitude of Lake Erie alone, quite apart from the other lakes, the undefended border dividing the United States and Canada strikes an imaginary horizontal line from the Niagara river in the east and westward to just south of Middle Island where it veers diagonally northwest between the oddly named Big Chicken Island (in Canadian waters) and North Bass Island in the state of Ohio. From a geographical aspect, taking a position from Port Clinton on the Ohio state main land, Rattlesnake Island, a mere 85 acres, lies some 10 to 12 miles notheast and in the shadow of North, Middle and South Bass Islands to the east, the latter being more commonly known as Put In Bay. Figure 4 shows the general layout of the islands, the boundary line and the position of Rattlesnake Island.

Historically, South Bass Island is probably the more notable of all the islands, except perhaps Rattlesnake Island simply for its name, which no doubt conjures up many an image to a vivid imagination. South Bass is the second largest of the islands and it was Put In Bay that Perry used as a base for his fleet, and from here that he sailed to fight his historic battle and win that famous victory over the British. In remembrance of that great occasion, South Bass is host to Perry's Victory and International Peace Memorial beneath which three American and three British officers who were killed in the battle, are buried. The monument was constructed between 1912 and 1915 to celebrate one hundred years of peace and was opened to the public in 1915. By 1931 a number of improvements had been made and a formal dedication of the memorial was held on 31st July 1931. On the 2nd June 1936, the monument became a National Monument under the administration of the National Park Service. The granite monument stands 352 feet above Lake Erie capped by an eleven ton bronze urn. The observation gallery offers a panoramic view

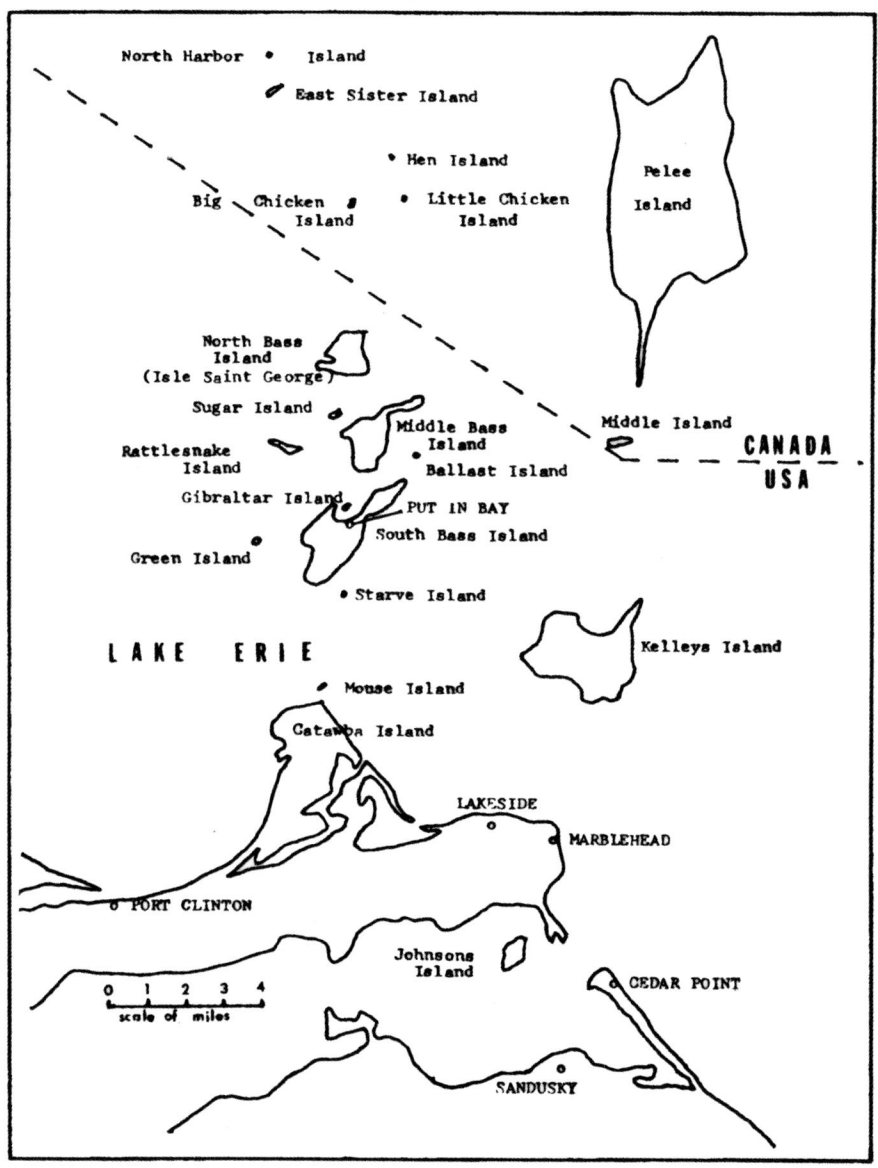

Figure 4   Lake Erie Islands

of western Lake Erie. The distance from Rattlesnake Island to Put In Bay is about two miles with the tiny piece of land between called Gibraltar Island at one time owned by a Civil War financier named Jay Cooke. The domed building on the eastern half of the island, commonly named Cooke's Castle was built by him as a summer residence. Cooke later sold the island to Franz Theodore Stone and it was eventually donated to the Ohio State University.

Approximately fifteen miles to the west of Rattlesnake Island lies West Sister Island (not shown on the map) which is a National Wildlife Refuge and a haven for many species of shore birds. It was close to this island that the Battle of Lake Erie came to its conclusion and the Americans gained control of Michigan, northern Ohio and the old northwest. To the left just off the western tip of South Bass lies Green Island where the lighthouse there has guided ships safely through the islands for decades. In the other direction, to the east is the legendary Starve Island. This tiny two acre dot of land is the site where it is reputed that a sailor starved to death after being shipwrecked and stranded there, though when this was supposed to have occurred, nobody knows. Starve is also known as Gull Island being a favourite nesting place for the local species of sea gull.

Also visible in a southerly direction is Catawba Point and Marblehead Peninsula. Marblehead Lighthouse situated at the entrance to Sandusky Bay dates back to 1812 and is the oldest lighthouse in continuous use on Lake Erie. Inside Sandusky Bay, off the south shore of Marblehead, lies Johnson's Island. In October 1861, the island was designated a Confederate prisoner of war camp and by 1863, when in full operation, as many as 2,600 Confederate officers and men were imprisoned there. Just off the northern tip of Catawba, near Miller's boat dock, is another tiny piece of land with the unusual name of Mouse Island, named for its small size and not because it was so infested with mice. The largest of the American islands boasting nearly three thousand acres is Kelleys Island, formerly known as Cunningham's Island until 1833 when the Kelley family took up residence, situated to the southeast and twice the size of South Bass. On this island glacial grooves, an after effect of the ice age activity, can be seen. Kelleys Island is also the site of Inscription Rock no less than 32 feet long by 21 feet wide, a pictographic history and proof of the Erie Indian Tribe's occupation of the island. Middle Island to the east is the nearest Canadian island, but the largest island in the lake is Pelee Island roughly ten miles northeastward at 36 square miles dwarfing Put In Bay's two square miles. Pelee is mainly farming country but is also renowned as an excellent fishing resort having been host to past Presidents Cleveland, Harding and Taft.

To the east of Middle Bass Island stands Ballast Island, where according to legend, Perry stopped to gather rocks along the shoreline for use as ballast on his ships, hence the name. During the latter part of the 19th century, the Bass Islands were known as wine islands due to the condusive climate in the area enabling the vines to flourish, resulting in large quantities of grapes, thus fine wines were produced. Although the advent of prohibition seriously affected the wine industry, today most of North as well as parts of Middle and South Bass are devoted to grape production.

The islands mentioned, are just a few of the total number within Lake Erie, on a clear day looking to the north, in the far distance more islands with the inspired names of Hen, Big Chicken and Little Chicken can be seen, and all of these are …..*in a single lake?*

3. The Erie Islands Postal Service

Of all the islands to be found within Lake Erie, Rattlesnake Island, marked by steep shoreline cliffs, is particularly significant and perhaps unique, not only for its unusual name, but in that for a limited number of years it was able to boast of being the first, and only location in the whole of the United States, to establish its very own airmail local post service to and from the Ohio mainland.

Somewhere between 1929 and 1932 the island was developed as a holiday home by the Toledo Scale Company president and industrialist Hubert Bennett. He was obviously a man of considerable affluence and astuteness, when one considers that during the late 20s and early 30s, much of America was reeling under the double blow of the Great Depression, and what was commonly known as the Dust Bowl, with the country's economy at rock bottom, and having suffered five years of the worst drought in American history. Hubert Bennett however, was also a man of vision and imagination, he spent no less than $250,000 building a residential cabin, guest accommodation, a harbour and last but not least, a landing strip for small aircraft which subsequently, was to prove invaluable. (Figure 5 shows some of the facilities) The landing strip ran directionally east - west and was 1,680ft long. A second north -south 950ft runway was constructed at a later date when a Catholic Order owned the island. Both airstrips were of grass, covering a smooth limestone base. Many trees, flowering plants and grapevines were imported onto the island along with various animal life, such as sheep, wild turkeys, ring-necked and golden pheasants, the latter eventually gave its name to the inn-cum-restaurant on the island. Mr Bennett died on September 8th 1951 but his legacy lives on.

Among Mr Bennett's staff was a versatile and much experienced gentleman by the name of Walter Lemke who was employed as caretaker of Rattlesnake Island from March 1945, and continued

Figure 5a The 4-bedroom South Lodge

Figure 5b The Golden Pheasant Inn

Figure 5c Living room fireplace of Main Lodge

Figure 5d Part of private harbour

Figure 5e Aerial view of island in winter

through to April 1953. Prior to taking up this important appointment, Walter had turned his hand to many occupations, he had been a farm hand, steel-mill worker, vineyard worker, commercial fisherman and a oiler-fireman aboard the steamship ferry "Chippewa" which made regular runs to the islands and Detroit. On taking up his post on Rattlesnake Island, with the assistance of his wife Ruth, Walter's tasks included keeping the grounds in good order and to maintain the log guest house, lodge-cum-restaurant, caretaker's house, the runway, a small powerhouse with gasoline generators for electric power plus a small yacht basin and its two vessels. (Electricity was later supplied by the Ohio Edison Co with the generators retained on standby for use in the event of a power failure, whilst telephone communication was eventually provided by the Northern Ohio Telephone Co.) One would imagine this would keep two people very busy, but no, Walter supplemented his caretaker's income by selling smoked fish and operating a string of 10 ice-fishing shanties during the popular winter ice-fishing season. During this time, apparently there were no telephones on the island and in case of emergency, the only way to get assistance was from the daily, but seasonal, passing of commercial fishing boats, or mirror signals to the Ford Tri-motor aircraft (later to become significant and important to Rattlesnake Island's survival) which passed overhead daily on its way from Port Clinton to South Bass Island. Details taken from Walter's personal notes indicate that in 1952 the island was bought for around $60,000 from the Bennett Estate by the Harbor Island Club, Inc., of Oak St. Cincinnati, for development of an exclusive sportsman's club. These plans actually failed to materialise and the island was again sold for $45,000 to a Catholic order run by Father Charles Haley, to use as a retreat for priests. At this point Walter Lemke writes that due to the difference of religion he was dismissed. In 1953, Walter subsequently became the first captain of the Ohio Division of Geological Survey research vessel, a position he held for 23 years until his retirement in 1976. Walter passed away in 1997 at the age of 91.

    The religious order occupied the island for only a short period before it was sold again to a syndicate headed by Mr Sanford T

Allen, president of the firm, Allen Travel Service, in Cleveland. By this time, the island's accommodation and recreation facilities had increased to include, in addition to the existing six-room lodge, a four-bedroom guest lodge, servants' quarters, and a house of entertainment complete with bar and kitchen. There also exists a cement and steel boat dock, a farmhouse normally occupied by the caretaker and his family, with dormitory rooms for no less than sixteen people. Allen eventually sold the island in 1959 for $100,000 to the eminent surgeon

Figure 6. *Walter R. Lemke*

James P. Frackelton, M.D. and Stockbroker, Robert C. Shull, who between them, operated a year-round lodge and resort facility for executive meetings, but also open to the public. The owners later attempted to convert the island into a private club, also, to develop a rehabilitation centre for heart disease, but they were unable to raise sufficient funds to establish the centre. The new incumbents were finding it increasingly difficult to operate the lodge and resort facilities and to make matters worse, unlike the nearby islands of North, Middle and Bass, who had secured a mailing contract with a small air transport company called Island Airlines, and recognised by the United States Post Office, there was no direct mailing service to and from the mainland to handle postal applications from prospective clients, and other general mail. Despite numerous requests, the Post Office steadfastly refused to provide any service, in fact, in its early days, it did not feel obliged to provide any delivery or collection service anywhere at all, anyone wishing to send mail, or expecting to receive any, were required to call at their local post office.

On the American mainland from 1844 onwards, a number of

private companies began providing a postal collection and delivery service, whereby for a small fee they would collect and deliver to and from a client's home or office. Most of the local post companies issued imperforate stamps which were affixed to the mail to indicate the fee had been paid. City posts generally charged one cent to deliver a letter to the Post Office which would also bear a government stamp, and two cents for intercity delivery although these letters bore only local stamps. The US Post Office was content to allow the local postal services to continue since it gave the impression they were offering an improved service. Unfortunately it soon became apparent that the local post was considerably better and more competitive than the Post Office. The Act of 1861 forced most of the local posts to discontinue except Boyd's Local Post of New York who went into the business of selling mailing lists and are still operating. Another was the now world famous Wells Fargo who, among other things, supply an armoured vehicle collection and delivery service to convey valuable cargo, and Hussey's who were permitted to continue for about twenty years longer due to the nature of their business. Other illegal postal services sprang up from time to time but these were quickly suppressed.

During this period things were happening around the Lake Erie islands. There was an ever increasing interest in the area with the result that by 1866 each of the Bass islands had its own post office. Put In Bay was the name given to the post office on South Bass which opened on 24th August 1860, whilst North Bass Island post office was established on 25th May 1864. However, on 2nd March 1874 it was changed to Isle Saint George although to all the local inhabitants it is still North Bass. On October 25th 1866, Middle Bass post office was born, but then, for some unknown reason on 1st December 1918 it was closed, only to be re-instated on 25th April 1919. The US Post Office continued to service these islands while Rattlesnake Island was consistently being ignored.

However, the delivery and collection of mail to and from the islands was not always straight forward, particularly during the winter months when journeys were extremely hazardous. Mail carriers used many different modes of transport according to the prevailing conditions. During the navigation season, mail and other supplies were conveyed to the islands by steamboat. When the lake began to freeze in the winter, other methods of overcoming the problems in reaching their destination had to be considered. From the 1st December to 31st March, the most difficult period of the year, the contract to carry mail to the islands was awarded to several men. When the ice forms on Lake Erie it is not skating rink smooth as one might imagine. It is in fact quite rough as a result of large chunks of ice breaking off and becoming trapped when the surrounding water re-freezes leaving ridges and uneven levels. During early winter and the coming of spring, open water appears together with areas of thin ice. With no barriers to break the force, strong winds whip over the ice and water and combined with the strong current, can push the ice causing it to form walls of solid ice 10ft. high or more. Because of this act of nature and the resulting obstacles, the route from A to B often became both hazardous and dangerous requiring transport to navigate a devious course.

When the ice was strong enough, a horse and sleigh were used, and many of the carriers tell stories of their experiences during the trips they made. One such carrier, by the name of Amos Hitchcock, was carrying two passengers and a large quantity of mail weighing several hundred pounds from Port Clinton on the mainland to Put In Bay with a horse and sleigh one winter's day, when he came upon a crack in the ice too wide to cross. The resourceful carrier apparently chopped out a very large slice of ice and used it to ferry the horse, sleigh, mail and the two passengers across the open expanse of water. Because the horses and sleighs would occasionally break through the ice, ropes, poles and hoisting equipment were usually carried to rescue them from the icy waters. Experienced island travellers found that when a horse fell into the icy water it quickly became numb and the only way to force it to struggle out was to tie a rope around its neck and choke it. The effect of this made the horse kick, during which time the men pulled on the rope, and if they were lucky, managed to retrieve the horse back on to firm solid ice. Sometimes, and I suspect most times, the men brought along a bottle of brandy or whiskey to keep themselves fortified against the bitter cold, maybe also, the horse was occasionally given a taste for warmth.

At times when the temperature had risen and the ice was not strong enough to support the weight of horse drawn transport or there were large expanses of water to cross, the mail carriers used a special kind of boat called an "ironclad". An ironclad was a strange looking boat specifically developed for the peculiar conditions to be faced. It began as an ordinary flat-bottomed rowing boat that was encased in metal to protect the wooden hull from the rough ice. It also had a pair of metal runners fixed to the underside so that it could be pulled over the ice. A typical ironclad was about fourteen feet long, oars were used to propel it in open water, although a sail was sometimes used when the wind was strong. Later an outboard motor provided power, but on firm ice, the carriers pulled the boat with ropes.

In the 1890s, on a trip between Middle Bass Island and Put In Bay, Lyndon and Ernest Hitchcock found the ice breaking up. They could not pull the boat or use the oars, so they had to push and shove the boat from ice floe to ice floe, often waist deep in ice cold water. So hazardous were some of the journeys that alas, occasionally a mail carrier gave his life serving the islanders. In January 1903, when George Morrison and Carl Totert set out from Catawba peninsula, they encountered thin ice, sadly, Totert fell through and disappeared beneath the water before Morrison could help him. His body was recovered in the Spring.

An article that appeared in the Cleveland Press in January 1923 vividly describes a journey between the mainland and South Bass Island. The reporter, one Fenney Smith relates how the ice "bowed" but did not break when the party walked on it. The carriers Arnold Burggraf and Maurice Arndt rowed in open water using oars and poles to push against the ice chunks or to break up the thin ice in front of the boat, the journey took two hours. It once took carrier Henry Enfers eight hours to cross the ice because it was too thin in many places to support his weight, thus forcing him to take a diverse and meandering route.

Most trips normally took about an hour, the schedule called for the carriers to leave Put In Bay at 9 a.m and to arrive at Catawba around 10.30 a.m. On the return trip, they would leave at about 12.30 p.m., this timetable was entirely dependant on the prevailing weather conditions.

By the 1920s, mail carriers had advanced from horse and sleigh in the winter to using cars and trucks, that is, when the ice was frozen solid, and was relatively smooth and thick enough to withstand the extra weight. The carriers generally used old topless cars, (sometimes with the doors removed) to reduce the weight and to make the cars safer. In the event that the vehicle suddenly broke through the ice, or began to sink in the soft ice, the occupants could jump out quickly. In January 1930, carriers Lee Miller and Cletus March were driving from Catawba to Put In Bay when their car became stuck in soft ice. The lighthouse keeper noticed their problem and notified the postmaster, William Schoor, at Put In Bay, who's prompt action of laying out planks of wood enabled them to get the car back on to safe ice.

And so, with the passage of time, thanks to the Ford Motor Company, the hazards of conveying supplies, mail and people to and from the Erie islands, were eased considerably with the advent of the Ford Tri-motor all metal aircraft. In addition to eventually becoming well known among the islanders and others as the "Tin Goose", it was to gain international recognition and fame. Although Henry Ford was interested in promoting air transportation and predicted a great future for it, he did not like flying. Charles Lindbergh was the first pilot to fly the "Tin Goose", Ford Tri-motor - N-7584, (later to become one of Island Airlines fleet of aircraft, see Figure 7) and it was in the summer of 1927, shortly after his return from Paris, following his historic solo crossing of the Atlantic ocean, that Lindbergh visited Dearborn Airport and took Ford up for his first and only time. Lindbergh was at the controls and Ford was in the co-pilot's seat. The picture, (see Figure 8) shows at left, Ford's Chief Engineer, William B. Mayo, Henry Ford boarding the aircraft, assisted by Lindbergh(helmeted) with Bill Stout behind and Edsel Ford, far right.

Figure 7

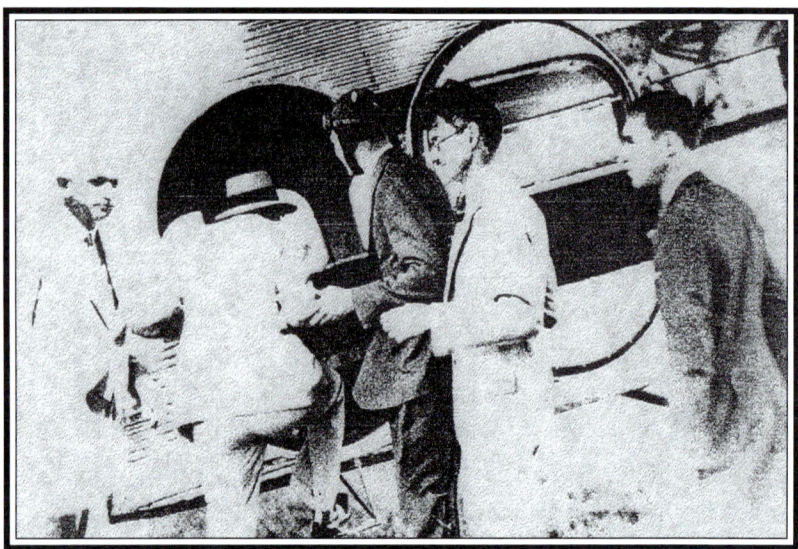

Figure 8

The Ford Tri-motor gained further recognition when Admiral Richard Byrd flew one of these now historic aircraft over the South Pole on November 28th 1929. The Ford motor car had achieved the merit of being the symbol of reliability and therefore many people had concluded that for such a reputable company to be building aircraft, it must surely be safe to fly as a passenger in their aeroplanes, and so it proved, although there were a few mishaps in later years.

Figure 9
The "Tin Goose" flown by Adm. Richard Byrd over the South Pole.

Figure 10
Shows the same aircraft later in use with Island Airlines.

4. The Erie Islands Aircraft (The Tin Goose)

The birth of the Ford Tri-motor can really be attributed to one William B. Stout, an engineer who had the skill and aptitude to design aircraft, albeit the designs were very much influenced by German expertise. However, Stout was a bold and astute salesman, having circulated a mimeographed letter to several leading manufacturers, appealing, rather with tongue-in-cheek, for them to part with $1,000, with the guarantee that they would definitely *not* get their money back. The response was that Stout raised no less than $20,000, including $1,000 each from Edsel and Henry Ford. These members of the Ford family became very interested in air transport, and in April 1925 the Ford Motor Company began an experimental air freight service between Detroit and Chicago. In August of the same year, Ford purchased the Stout Metal Airplane Company. Stout's aircraft designs had all been based on a single engine, but the introduction of the lightweight Wright air-cooled radial engine led Stout and his design team to re-think and consider the manufacture of a more powerful and reliable aircraft fitted with three engines, thus the Ford Tri-motor was born.

The first Ford Tri-motor, the 3-AT (the letters denoting Air Transport), was not a particularly attractive looking aircraft, plus the positioning of the engines meant that it was unable to land safely without engine power. This model actually only made three flights and seemed to be doomed from the start following a fire in the factory which destroyed this and other planes, it also saw the end of Stout's design work with Ford. The unfortunate turn of events may have been a blessing in disguise, for it prompted work to begin on the 4-AT, an improved model which was to become the foundation of the classic Ford Tri-motor. The first 4-AT made its maiden flight on 11th June 1926 and became very popular among many airlines mainly due to its ever growing reputation for stability, sturdy construction, its ability to fly well on two engines and even to maintain level flight on just a single engine. It also had the added advantage of operating from grass and dirt airstrips. However, in the summer of 1928, a more advanced aircraft was to make its appearance having been equipped with the new Pratt and Whitney 420-hp Wasp engine, this was the 5-AT which became the most famous of the Ford Tri-motor designs. By the time Ford ceased producing aircraft in 1933, no less than 199 Tri-motors had been built and served more than one hundred airlines around the world.

Figures 11 and 12

Figure 13 Ford Tri-motor in flight

Although there was considerable interest in establishing a regular air service to the islands, the arrival on the scene of the later Tri-motor model given the nickname "Tin Goose" was not immediate. A small airline owned by the Parker Brothers which operated from Sandusky, arranged an exploratory flight to the islands. At the controls was one "Barnstormer" Milton Hershberger who, in February 1929, landed on the ice near Gibraltar Island and taxied into the bay. Also on board was the Rev. Joseph E. Maerder, pastor of the Catholic churches on Put In Bay and Kelleys Island. A meeting was held with the Mayor, T. B. Alexander and other islanders to consider the possiblility of building a landing strip on South Bass. Shortly after these discussions, Milton Hershberger left Parker Brothers Airline and set up his own company called Erie Isle Airways. The first flight of the new airline took place on November 11th 1930, flying a Waco bi-plane. Thus began a regular scheduled air service to Put In Bay, Middle Bass and North Bass. The pilot, Hershberger, frequently assisted the mail carriers by conveying the postmen and their cargo when icy conditions were particularly bad.

Figure 14 Rev. Maerder arriving for meeting

Lee Miller, one of the courageous mail carriers who had previously driven a car across the ice to deliver mail and goods etc, along with John Parker and the Erie Isles Airways, put in a bid for the mail contract covering the winter period of 1931 - 1932, this was subsequently awarded to Erie Isle Airways. The route, known as a star route was from Sandusky to Kelley's Island, Put In Bay, Middle Bass, North Bass, and back to Sandusky. The regular first class postage rate applied, not the airmail rate as one would assume, even though the mail was carried by aircraft. The airmail service was offered only from December 1st 1931 to March 31st 1932. During the summer months, the mail was usually carried by boat, except to North Bass, which had no regular boat service. An airmail service to North Bass began on 16th July 1931. In 1932, the air route for the mail contract was amended whereby flights began and ended at Port Clinton instead of Sandusky. The service from Port Clinton continued thereafter all year round.

Milton Hershberger operated the air service between the mainland and the Erie islands from 1930 to 1953 and became a prominent figure in the history of the islands. Having established a successful air service, he gained national recognition during the years after World War II when passenger air travel was rapidly expanding. Born in Anderson, Indiana on 29th December 1901, Hershberger was taught to fly by one Erret Williams, himself a barnstormer, in 1923, and made his first solo flight in the summer of that year at Berry Field in Richmond, Indiana. Between 1924 and 1926, he barnstormed throughout Ohio, Indiana and Illinois. During 1927 and '28 Hershberger was airport manager at Sandusky, Ohio, and it was during this time that he realised how useful an air service could be to the people living on the Erie Islands, particularly during the winter months when travel across the ice could be so hazardous and dangerous. However, in the interim period up to the beginning of his airline, between 1928 and 1930 Hershberger worked as a pilot and test pilot for several companies, some of which eventually merged to become United Airlines. Milton Hershberger was an accomplished pilot and whilst in the employ of Chicago's Stinson Airport as chief pilot for Art Killip's passenger service he had the opportunity to compete in the 1930 National Air Show and won the "dead stick" landing competition three days running. Later that same year he learned of the sinking of the Lake Island ferry "Mascot" and that its passengers were stranded on the mainland, Milton flew back to Ohio to transport them to their homes.

Things were progressing quite well for Milton Hershberger flying his Waco bi-plane and serving the islanders. A fire at Chicago Municipal Airport which destroyed several aircraft hangars resulted in the sale of salvaged engines thus enabling Hershberger to replace the water-cooled engine. However, his aircraft did not offer

"Barnstormer" Milton ("Red") Hershberger, who started Island Airline operation in 1929.

Figure 15
"Barnstormer" Milton Hershberger at the controls

Figure 16
Shows an interesting cover signed by Milton Hershberger.

enclosed protection from the elements and a journey during the heart of winter could be extremely cold and uncomfortable. Nevertheless, the popularity of the service he provided saw a considerable increase in demand to carry larger quantities of freight and more passengers and with it came the need for better and larger aircraft with enclosed cabins, thus offering prospective passengers a little more comfort. Hershberger turned his attention to the up and coming Ford Tri-motor which he believed would solve his immediate problems, but alas, at $5,500 a time they were beyond his means. His fortunes changed however, when in 1934 he heard that a Tri-motor had crashed after running out of fuel, near Pittsburgh, and so snapped it up for a mere $2,500. Throughout his career Hershberger travelled far and wide to purchase used Tri-motors, even to Alaska, the Dominican Republic and Cuba.

By 1935 Hershberger had acquired no fewer than five Tri-motors and with the increasing success of his air service to and from the Erie islands, he decided to change the name of his Company to Island Airways. Although they were an improvement on the earlier planes, the Tri-motor was still a cold and draughty experience, but thankfully the flight between the various islands lasted only a few minutes and was therefore tolerable. The aircraft could accommodate twelve to fifteen passengers, but like the structure itself, the seats were also metal and bolted to the floor of the plane. In addition to flying residents of the islands plus summertime and winter visitors back and forth, during the pheasant hunting and ice-fishing seasons, his most frequent cargo, in addition to the mail, was wine from the Lonz vineyards on Middle Bass Island, and wineries established on other islands. He also carried farm animals which was no doubt delightful for the passengers, plus a variety of appliances, groceries and other essential supplies. On occasions his aircraft became an ambulance or even a flying hearse. The airline generally, had a good safety record, but as with this form of travel, and indeed, with any other come to that, there is always an element of risk that one might suffer mild or serious injury, and on occasions injuries that could be fatal. In May 1934, with the now very experienced Hershberger at the controls, a Standard bi-plane fell into the water near Lakeside. Hershberger, along with seven bags of mail, was rescued by a commercial fishing boat which thankfully was close by. On December 29th 1937, another Standard bi-plane crashed near Starve Island, sadly three passengers were drowned. On July 31st 1954 a Ford Tri-motor crashed at Kelleys Island and in later years other misfortunes befell this aircraft design despite its record of stability and reliabilty. Whether these events were as a result of pilot error, or whatever, there is no doubt that the "Tin Goose" was, and still is, a popular aircraft offering the adventurous a thrill and excitement rarely available in today's air travel.

    In 1953, Milton Hershberger sold his airline to Travelair Taxi, Inc., a subsidiary of Sandusky Airport, Inc., run by Ralph Dietrick, for $95,000 who promptly changed the name to "Island Airlines", (see Figure 17) and although he probably didn't know it at the time, was to become an integral part of the now world famous Rattlesnake Island local airmail postal service. The airline achieved the distinction of being the "Shortest Scheduled Airline in the World" and carried many thousands of avid visitors to the islands every year. It was reckoned that when for example, the plane took off from say, Put In Bay en route to Middle Bass, reaching an altitude of just five hundred feet, the flight took only three minutes and the wheels of the plane would still be spinning from the take-off, when it landed.

Figure 17
Island Airlines and the Ford Tri-Motor

Milton Hershberger meanwhile had purchased Urb's Café, situated in Port Clinton, in 1951. He and his wife devoted all their time into operating it. Hershberger had a long and eventful life and passed away in 1987. Incidentally, Urb's Café is now Zs Tin Goose Saloon.

Ralph Dietrick, a World War II veteran command pilot, had been providing an air service from Sandusky to Kelley and Pelee islands alongside Hershberger's Island Airways service. Dietrick consolidated the two airlines at the Sandusky terminal, but around nine years later he moved the whole operation to Port Clinton and changed the name to Island Airlines, at the same time he sold off the Kelley and Pelee routes.

By the mid-1960s Dietrick's fleet of aircraft included three Ford

Tri-motors, an old Boeing 247 thought to be the only remaining flyable plane of its type, four Cessnas, a Mooney and a Piper Cherokee. The old Ford Tri-motors were the main attraction for flying enthusiasts, from all over America and countries around the world, people came to see, touch and ride in a "Tin Goose" of Island Airlines. In the summertime when the normal islands population of 800 swelled to over 10,000 visitors, it was impossible to obtain a ride without a reservation. Such was the excitement and desire just to ride a Tri-motor, people didn't mind in the least how hot, noisy and uncomfortable the trip might be, air conditioning consisted of an open window with the possibility of a few delightful odours, such as stale fish thrown in for good measure.

Ralph Dietrick, president of Sky Tours, Inc.,

Figure 18
Shows pilot Ralph Dietrick at the controls.

The fare for this wonderful experience, a round trip from South Bass to Port Clinton was a mere four dollars. If you were planning to visit any other island, you paid the pilot the extra fare. Records show that in 1967, the world's shortest scheduled airline carried 65.000 passengers, 300,000 pounds of freight and 150,000 pounds of commercial and philatelic mail. Since as previously mentioned, planes never really flew above 500 feet, the most reliable guide to weather conditions for flying was "Perry's Monument". Dietrick maintained that this was all the weather equipment he needed. "If we can see the top of the monument, that is ceiling enough for

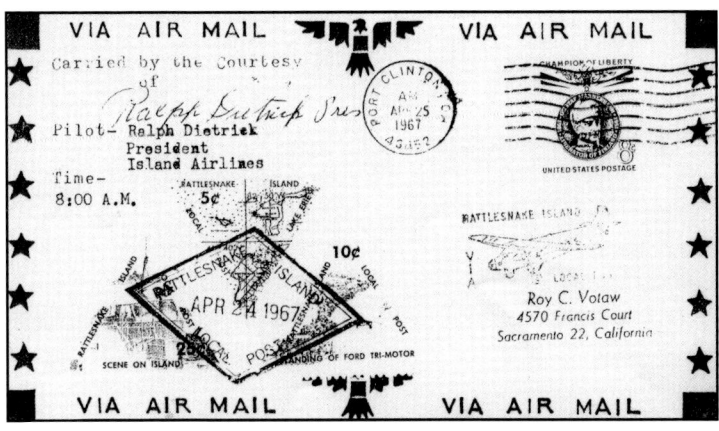

Figure 19
Shows a cover signed by Ralph Dietrick carried on one of his flights.

the Tri-motors." Maintenance and upkeep of the Tri-motors was a relatively simple task, control cables all ran outside the planes and were easy to inspect and repair, the engines were also fairly straightforward to work on. According to the maintenance crews, the hardest job was removing the smell of fish from the cabins after the fishermen had flown their catches home.

Previously, Milton Hershberger had managed to store away a reserve supply of ailerons, rudders, stabilizers and corrugated skin pieces for the Tri-motors, so there was a good chance that the Tin Goose would continue flying for some time to come. Ralph Dietrick reckoned that he had enough parts for another 15 years of life in the old aircraft. However, in 1973 Island Airlines and its parent company, Sky Tours, Inc., was sold to David Haberman together with some other investors, unfortunately, by this time only one Tri-motor was still airworthy. Then sadly, on 1st July 1977 the last Tri-motor crashed on take-off, severely injuring the pilot, Dave Martin, but only slightly harming a couple of passengers. Such was the sadness at the loss of this famous old carrier, from all over the world, fans of Island Airlines appealed to Haberman to "Re-build her and let her fly again." Letters and donations poured in and after much searching, and at a cost of $300,000 Kal Aero in Kalamazoo, MI, rebuilt the plane but with a few modifications. According to a paper report, the restored Tin Goose was due to return to a champagne welcome at Port Clinton Tuesday 1st April 1980, where a host of newspaper and television reporters were waiting, only to be disappointed. Due to fog, an erratic radio and faulty compass, the plane was forced to land at Hillsdale, Michigan. Pilots Harold Hauck, who actually flew Tri-motors longer than any other pilot, and Dave Martin, again set off thinking they could find a clear route east and then veer right at Adrian, Michigan, following highways and railway tracks. Following in another small aircraft, was David Haberman, who pointed out that in the old days, this rather hit and miss method of direction was the way it was done. As the plane approached a town it would drop down to read the name on the water tower to establish where they were.

Figure 20
A "Tin Goose" flies past Perry's Monument on South Bass Island.

Although the newly restored Tin Goose had now been fitted with a radio and up-to-date navigational aids, flying her was still a risky adventure. Halfway to Adrian, Haberman lost sight of the Goose and neither could see the highway except for breaks in the fog. Since the Tri-motor could only do 80 miles per hour,

Haberman in his faster Cessna radioed that he would turn right and the Goose should go left to avoid a mid-air collision. Eventually the Tin Goose arrived at Hillsdale but Haberman had to circle in and out of the fog several times before finding the airstrip and land. The Tin Goose finally arrived at Port Clinton at 3 p.m. on Thursday 3rd April where someone managed to find a bottle of champagne for a toast. When questioned about the Tin Goose's future, Dave Haberman said that the plane is stronger now because of new alloys and weighed 141 pounds less because they had cleaned the grease and dirt out of her plus a 1927 dime that someone dropped whilst they were building her.

The Tin Goose still flies today although it is restricted to flying only over land, passengers are not allowed over water. In fact it is now limited to taking off from the mainland airport, circling a few times then landing, although it occasionally attends fairs and special functions. Nevertheless, the Tin Goose, one of the early pioneers of passenger flight, made many people happy and left thousands with treasured memories. Flights to the islands are now undertaken by more modern aircraft so perhaps the flight time is now down to two minutes instead of three.

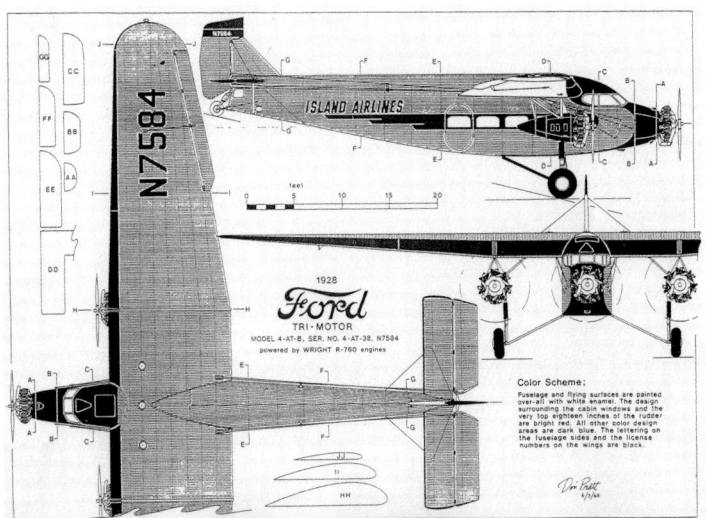

Figure 21

5. Rattlesnake Island Local Airmail Post

Meanwhile, although air services to the Erie islands was flourishing and inhabitants of some of the larger areas had enjoyed a regular postal service for several years, even though the air service included scheduled visits to Rattlesnake Island for commercial purposes, the United States Post Office continued to refuse a mail service to be included in the contract set up with other islands. James P. Frackelton M.D., who, in addition to practising medicine full time, and who also owned the Cleveland Stamp & Coin Co. during the 1960s, made frequent applications to the United States Postal Authority for a mail service, but all to no avail. That is, until through his lifelong collecting interest in United States postage stamps and association with Herman J Herst Jr, he became aware of the successful application by Herman Herst Jr for a local postal service at Shrub Oak, New York, in 1952. Mr Herst's researches revealed that Title 18 of the U.S. Code permitted an individual to establish a local post service in areas to which the 1862 service covering home and office did not apply. In order to make certain that no regulations were likely to be breached, Mr Herst's lawyer wrote to the Solicitor-General of the United States Post Office to establish whether the law was still valid. Needless to say, he was delighted to find that it was. However, the Post Office insisted that although local postage was permissible, mail would not be accepted without an official stamp being affixed. The Post Office also decreed that no local post stamp should be placed in the upper right hand corner where the official stamp normally belonged and that no cancellation marks were permitted, to prevent re-use of the local post stamp, that might be similar to the official cancelling. The Shrub Oak local mail service continued unhindered for many years.

Once Mr Herst's success became known, Dr Frackelton wasted no time in formally submitting his application, again citing Title 18 of the United States Code. At last, after a long and arduous battle, the Post Office finally conceded that the existing airmail postal service to the islands could now embrace Rattlesnake Island. Bearing in mind that the new incumbents had taken over the island in 1959, it wasn't until 1966 that the Post Office gave its approval. However, restrictions applied, in addition to those already mentioned, whereby the local post stamps affixed to mail were legal only for the journey from the island to the mainland post office at Port Clinton, Ohio, where it entered the United States mailstream.

The very first set of stamps were issued on 27th August 1966, designed by Dr Frackelton and printed by the Mueller Printing Company of Cleveland, Ohio of which Henry Prokopek was President. In most instances the stamp designs were derived from features associated with the island, such as fish, birds and other wildlife etc. However, the initial stamps were printed in three denominations and rectangular in shape. The three values were 5c, depicting a map of the island in black with red text, for use on airmail postcards, 10c portraying an aerial view of the island with a Tri-motor in flight, printed in green with black text, being the rate for airmail letters, and 25c showing a harbour scene in blue and again with black text, intended for use on airmail parcels. In fact the picture used for the 25c stamp is of the United States Coast Guard docking before disembarking to enjoy a cup of free coffee in the island's kitchen, which apparently was a regular occurrence. Shown at Figure 22 are the three perforated stamps of the first issue on a postally used cover in rectangular format and the second issue of the same design but triangular.

This first issue and all subsequent stamps were printed in perforate and imperforate formats and in sets of three, except for 1972, when an additional 25c stamp was printed making a set of four, and an additional single stamp issued on 27th August 1986 to commemorate the 20th anniversary of the Rattlesnake Island local post.

Shortly after the first stamps were issued it was rumoured that the proofs of the stamps were put into circulation, but according to Dr Frackelton, in an interview with long time collector and exhibitor of Rattlesnake Island postal history, Bob Fritz, the sole intention was to issue stamps in the two formats only and no

Figure 22

proofs were ever made available to collectors. It is also alleged that some less scrupulous dealers of Rattlesnake Island Local Posts are offering purported printing errors of the first issue of stamps, such as horizontal imperforate pairs. Collectors should be very wary when considering purchasing supposed errors. Dr Frackelton further stated that, "Since there was no government control over the printing of the stamps, printing errors are really not defined for private printing." Therefore, the die-cut process for perforating this issue meant that a perforating error was virtually impossible, and certainly no deliberate errors had been created for philatelic purposes. However, this was not to say that it would not be a relatively simple matter for someone to take an imperforate sheet of stamps and create what would appear to be a credible perforating error. There are definitely no acknowledged legitimate errors for the first issue, but there are distinct colour varieties between the first and second printings of the 1966 issue. The second printing came about when Dr Frackelton was apparently disappointed in the pale colouring of the first issue and ordered a second printing to be processed with the result that the stamps have deeper and bolder colours, although the 5c denomination is difficult to distinguish except that there may be a suggestion of an orange tinge in the red text element of the design and the grey shade can be seen to be darker when placed beside the first issue. For these issues the same set of plates were used, but after completion of the printing process, the plates were destroyed, as was the case after each susequent stamp issue. No one knows for sure how many stamps were printed each time, although it has been said that 32,000 of each denomination were available for use and for distribution to collectors, but according to a handwritten response to a collector's enquiry, by the first postmistress, Mrs Lilian Busch, about 20,000 were printed, which means there are fewer stamps available to collectors thus making them much sought after. There was however, one notable major colour error on the 25c denomination second printing where the stamp has a bright green appearance. (see Figure 23) Most errors or colour shifts occurred between 1966 and 1969 but several only really came to light in 1974. Details of the varieties can be found in the separate catalogue listing.

The first issue of Rattlesnake Island stamps was less than four months old, and news of these new stamps had travelled far and wide among stamp collectors, when, in a telephone conversation with Dr Frackelton on the 9th December, followed by a confirmation letter dated 12th December, the United States Post Office Department

Figure 23

issued an order to the Port Clinton Post Office stating that the stamps being used by Rattlesnake Island Local Post violate Section 475 of Title 18, U.S. Code and as of December 9th 1966 matter bearing such stamps may not be accepted for mailing. Because of this rather sudden decision on the part of the U.S. Post Office, it is likely that the second printing of the first issue was used less on mail than the first paler coloured printing. The implied reason for the ban was that the stamps were too attractive and might be confused with the normal U.S. postage, although this was later denied by the Post Office. However, having already won the first round, so to speak, with the introduction of the first Rattlesnake Island stamps, Dr Frackelton was certainly not going to give up now, and in correspondence by his legal adviser to the Post Office Department's General Counsel, requested that triangular stamps and a diamond shaped logo be recognised and accepted as an alternative to the previously issued rectangular stamps.

In a rather long and protracted letter in true civil service fashion, the General Counsel replied in the following manner:

'This is in reply to your letter relative to the use of triangular and diamond shaped stickers on mail matter carried between Rattlesnake Island and Port Clinton, Ohio. You ask this office to authorise the issuance of private stickers of triangular or diamond shape to be used as stamps by the private express operating between Rattlesnake Island and Port Clinton.

The Post Office Department does not approve or authorise the use or issuance of any stickers or stamps other than those it issues. Matter bearing private stamps or stickers is accepted by the post office if the stickers are not deemed imitations of postage stamps, or in form and design like postage stamps. Matter bearing a triangular or diamond shaped sticker (an adhesive as distinguished from an embossed device) which is not otherwise deceptively similar in appearance to a postage stamp, and which is not so placed on an envelope so that it is easily taken to be postage indicia when considered either alone or in combination with other markings or cancelling devices, probably would be accepted for delivery by the post office. We point out that by Section 2501 of Title 39, U.S. Code, Congress has authorised the Postmaster

General to issue stamps in the form and design he deems necessary. Accordingly, the Department may in the future issue triangular or diamond shaped stamps. We also wish to point out that the final administrative decision whether any stamp is to be deemed the similitude of a United States stamp is made by the United States Secret Service, and not by the Post Office Department. Accordingly, even though this Department may not believe a triangular stamp violates the United States Criminal Code, that decision is not binding upon the Secret Service.'

The letter then goes on to say:

'The Department now supplies airmail envelopes bearing embossed triangular postage indicia. The Department will not accept for mailing matter bearing printed or embossed triangular designs similar thereto.

We have also read the sequal to Rattlesnake Island Local Post. We concede the stamps considered were attractive. We deny any implication the stamps were not acceptable because they were "too attractive." We also deny that it was stated that triangular stamps would be satisfactory under all conditions. At best it was stated that since, so far as was known, no triangular shaped stamps had ever been issued by this Department, triangularity would be an element considered in determining their acceptability to the Department.'

You did not furnish any of the examples of the triangular stickers you propose to issue, or advised us of the manner in which they are used. Accordingly, we cannot advise you whether this Department would be willing to accept mail bearing such stickers.'

During the period of these exchanges, even though the practice of affixing a local post stamp was forbidden, the mail continued to flow from the island, identifiable by the distinctive diamond shaped cancel with a hand written "Fee paid" entered beside it. This was known as the stampless period and lasted from December 9th 1966 until January 22nd 1967. The bulk of the "stampless" covers carry the Rattlesnake Island diamond cancellation date of December 30th 1966 as this was the date mailings were sent to collectors, who's numbers were growing rapidly as interest in the island's stamps spread virtually worldwide. This was a duty that befell the island's first postmistress, Mrs Lillian Busch, to announce the First Day of Issue date for the new triangular second issue of stamps, January 23rd 1967. There are other cancellation dates during the stampless period, which are very scarce. Figure 24 shows two covers from the stampless period, one bearing the December 30th 1966 cancellation, the other, rather more scarce shows January 12th 1967 in the diamond logo and January 13th 1967 in the Port Clinton circular date stamp.

Figure 24

Almost immediately after the first issue of triangular stamps which carried the same designs and denominations as the rectangular issue of August 27th 1966, on the 30th January 1967, Dr Frackelton's legal adviser submitted details of the proposed new stamps and diamond shaped logo to the United States Treasury Department for formal approval. On the 7th March a letter was sent by that Department effectively confirming acceptance of the revised designs. The basis of the letter was as follows:

'Reference is made to your letter dated January 30th 1967, and its attachments, relative to the legality of certain stamps used by the Rattlesnake Island Local Post.

As you are aware, section 474, title 18, United States Code, prohibits making any engraving, photograph, print or impression in the likeness of any obligation or security of the United States, or any part thereof. The term "obligation or other security of the United States" is defined by section 8, title 18, United States Code to include cancelled or uncancelled United States postage stamps. Section 481, title 18, United States Code, prohibits, among other things, the making of any engraving, photograph, print or impression in the likeness of any obligation or security of any foreign government, or any part thereof. The term "obligation or other security of any foreign government" is defined by title 18, United States code, section 15 to include uncancelled postage stamps of any foreign government, whether or not demonetized.'

The letter then goes on to say:

'It is the opinion of this Office, in whch the Office of the General Counsel concurs, that the reproductions of the triangular shape Rattlesnake Island Local Post stamps are not in sufficient similitude to any United States or foreign postage stamp to be prohibited by the foregoing statutes.

With reference to the post mark of Rattlesnake Island Local Post appearing on the attachments submitted with your letter, section 503, title 18, United States Code prohibits, among other things, the manufacture, possession or use of any counterfeit post marked stamps or impressions thereof, with intent to make them appear as genuine postmarks. However, since the post mark appearing on the attachments submitted with your letter is not similar to United States post marks, and is not being used with intent to make it appear that such post mark is genuine, there would appear to be no objection to its use.'

The foregoing opinion does not preclude the Post Office Department from making objection to the stamps for reasons other than their similitude to United States stamps. Further, in the event the Post Office Department should, at some future time, issue triangular adhesive stamps, then this department may find it necessary to re-examine our position in this matter.'

Having now satisfied the authorities, printing of the second issue could proceed unhindered and the triangular stamps were issued in sheets of 20 in both perforate and imperforate format, and for the first time, with plate numbers. The considerable demand for the new issue of triangular stamps, and because of the increased popularity of this unique tiny island's situation, Mrs Busch was kept extremely busy dealing with and fulfilling some 12,000 orders from every country around the world, except, oddly enough, Russia and the People's Republic of China. Today, the 10c triangular stamp is relatively scarce as a large quantity of sheets were destroyed by water damage.

Figure 25
Mrs Busch displaying stamps and covers

Approximately a month after the second issue became available, a curious thing happened which at first, nobody could explain. The post office on the island began receiving 'Care' packages from the then Eastern Bloc country of Hungary. These packages contained food, clothes and personal hygiene items along with Hungarian postage stamps, the latter were sent to be traded for Rattlesnake Island stamps. Mrs Busch duly obliged and sent Rattlesnake Island stamps as requested. The packages continued to arrive on the island and stamps continued to be exchanged, but the mystery as to why this was happening, remained.

The mystery was eventually resolved by none other than Dr Frackelton himself when enquiries revealed that the TV show, *'The Huntley-Brinkley Report'*, had broadcast a four minute interlude on their programme about the problems that Rattlesnake Island had experienced in fighting the United States Post Office to firstly obtain a regular mail service to and from the island, and secondly, to find a suitable stamp that did not contravene United States Post Office regulations. The TV programme likened the circumstances to that of a 'David and Goliath' battle and had declared that little Rattlesnake Island - 'David' - had fought the United States federal bureaucracy - 'Goliath' - and won. It transpired that for some strange reason a Budapest TV station, having come across this item which they obviously assumed would interest the viewers, translated and broadcast the story of how the revolutionaries on Rattlesnake Island in the 'Erie Sea' had fought the United States government and won. The TV station however, omitted to mention that the whole incident was to do with securing a mail service. The Hungarian people took sympathy on the 'repressed islanders' and so decided to send their 'Care' packages to the courageous revolutionaries who had beaten the capitalist government. And so the mystery was solved and Dr Frackelton believes that many Rattlesnake Island stamps now lie in albums and scrapbooks gathering dust, right across Hungary.

In general the stamps of Rattlesnake Island were colourful and very attractive, both the perforate and imperforate issues bore full gum, in most cases they depicted flora, fauna or scenes from the island, although in a few instances subjects were taken from photographs. The 1968 set of three stamps also saw the first use of a handstamp showing a Ford Tri-motor with the words 'Rattlesnake Island' set above the aircraft, the word 'via' positioned vertically in front of the plane and 'Local Post' beneath and towards the back of the plane. Details of the various handstamps used are set out elsewhere. About the time when Dr Frackelton was considering the designs for the 1969 stamps, a friend had submitted some pictures for consideration and possible use as subjects for the set. Having looked through the pictures Dr Frackelton

*Figure 26
Midge Christiansen*

particularly liked a photograph that he thought was quite touching. It showed a father standing with his daughter on the beach at sunset. The picture was subsequently selected for the 25c stamp. Since the intention, as has already been mentioned, was to depict aspects of the island on the stamps, one could be forgiven for believing that the beach scene was on the island. The truth of the matter is that, indeed it is an island scene at sunset as stated on the stamp, but it was in the Bahamas. The picture was actually taken by Midge Christiansen at Man-O-War Cay in the Bahama Islands.

Overleaf (see Figure 27) is a copy of the letter signed by Dr Frackelton, to Mrs Christiansen together with a print of the stamp used, thanking her for the use of the photograph and the return of same.

A new issue of the now much sought after stamps appeared each year with the original face value of each of the set of three remaining until 1974 when the values were increased to 20c, 30c and 50c. From the 1973 issue, all stamps were printed by the company - Great Lakes Lithography Co. of Cleveland, Ohio. Perforated stamps were perf 11¾. Dr Frackelton designed the stamps from 1966 to 1972. For the latter issue, the seventh, the 25c stamp, printed perforate and imperforate, portrayed Perry's Monument.

```
JAMES P. FRACKELTON, M.D.
26410 CENTER RIDGE ROAD
WESTLAKE, OHIO  44145
Phone 835-0104

Apr. 15, 1970



Mrs. R. J. Christiansen
20184 Beach Cliff
Rocky River, Ohio 44116

Dear Midge:
        Finally got your picture back and
am enclosing it together with one of the slides.
This shot has been very successful with lot of
comments and you are to be congratulated on
your photography.

        You mentioned to me that you would
find it easy to remount this as I see it was
taken out of the mounting. Did you give me
more than one slide? If so, I will check
further for it. Thanks again.

                        Sincerely,

                        Jim Frackelton

JF:d
encl.
```

Figure 27

Figure 28
Dr James Frackelton

Two stamps of this design and denomination were actually printed, only the wording differs in that one bears the words 'Perry's Monument' whilst the other bears the word 'Sightseeing'. Both stamps are from the same sheet with the different wording alternating across the sheet.

Although Dr Frackelton was the inspiration for the stamps at the outset, little is known about the individuals involved over the years except that from 1973 to 1977 the stamps were designed by Bernice Kochan, these were artists drawings of the island scenes. Following this period, Trisha Marcum designed the 1978 issue and Robert Eisenbarth the issues from 1979 until the final set of stamps depicting owls, in 1989, except the 1983 issue, again taken from photo-graphs. Whereas the stamps had usually comprised a set of three except the 1972 when four were printed, on 27th August 1986, a special 20th Anniversary single stamp was issued to commemorate twenty years of local airmail postal service. This was also designed by Robert Eisenbarth and was issued in a special souvenir folder.

Figure 29
Robert Eisenbarth

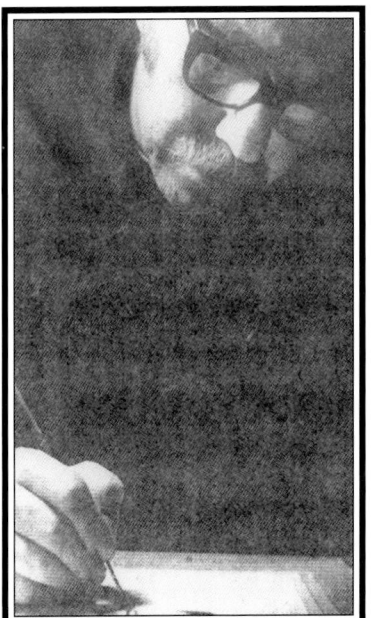

Figure 30
Robert Eisenbarth working on stamp designs

6. Postal Administration People

Around the time that Dr Frackelton and his associates bought Rattlesnake Island, the island population consisted of only four people, Mrs Lillian Busch who was to become the first postmistress, her husband Charles, appointed caretaker and general factotum, and their two children. During the time that the children attended school in Port Clinton, they collected the island mail each school day from Port Clinton post office.

The introduction of the local post on the island transformed the Busch family lifestyle almost overnight, when word travelled like lightning among stamp collectors, not only in the United States, but throughout the world. Demand for the stamps kept Mrs Busch extremely busy, writing letters addressing envelopes, all by hand, and ensuring the correct stamp orders were fulfilled. In addition to the ever increasing popularity of the stamp issues, Mrs Busch also served as chef and hostess to the island's owners and the executive guest visitors who called in at the Golden Pheasant Restaurant to dine during fishing or hunting expeditions.

Figure 31 Mrs Lillian Busch

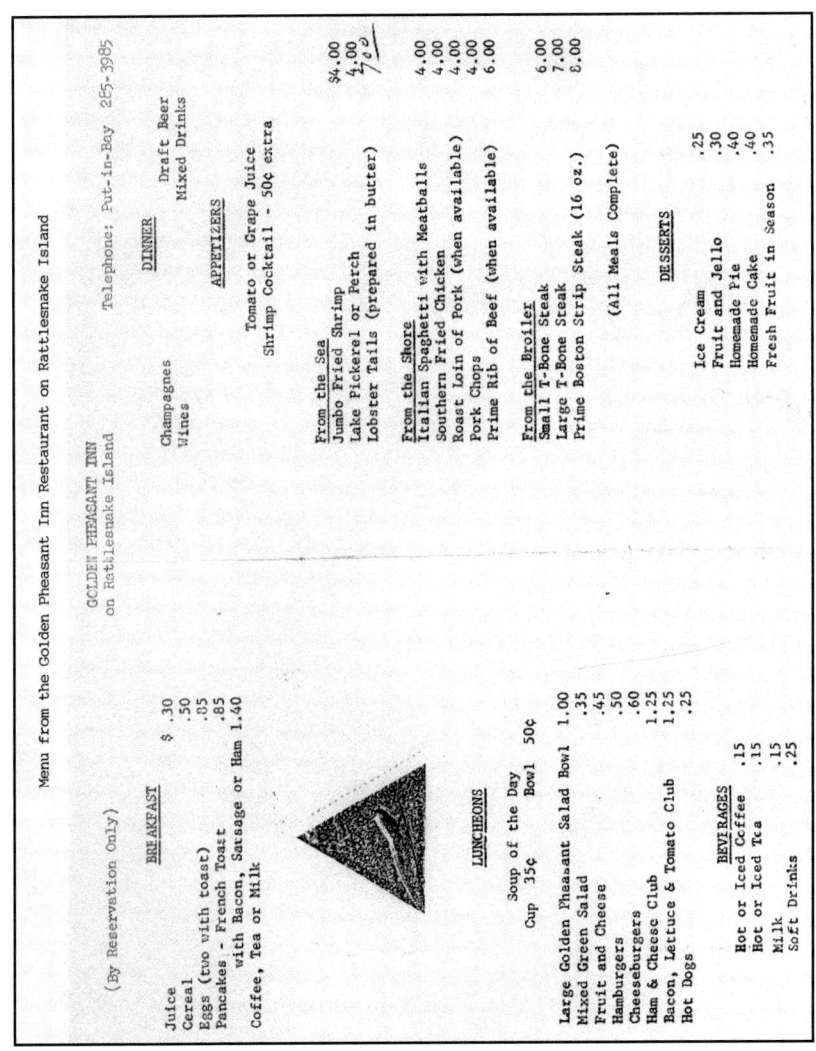

Figure 32 A typical menu

Charles Busch meanwhile, acted as guide around the island, in addition to ensuring the general upkeep of the lodges and other buildings as well as the grounds and sporting facilities. Charles also assisted in transporting the mail from the island post office to the waiting aircraft. Figure 33 shows Charles handing a bag of

mail to Ralph Dietrick, the pilot of the Ford Tri-motor - the "Tin Goose", whilst Figure 34 shows stamps being sold at Port Clinton Airport.

Figure 33

Figure 34

In 1970 the island was sold to businessman Dallas "Dutch" Biechele who not only carried out extensive repair work to the northeast dock and marina, but also stocked the island with pineapple and banana wine for parties and in 1972 the Golden Pheasant restaurant was opened to visitors. However, during the transition period Dr Frackelton continued to design and have printed the 1971 and 1972 stamp issues. At the time of the transfer of ownership the Busch family moved off the island and Mrs Dorothy Kelley succeeded Mrs Busch as postmistress and her husband Gene Kelley (no not *that* Gene Kelly) was now caretaker. Figure 35 shows Mr and Mrs Kelly on the island as postmistress and caretaker. The Kelley family remained on the island until 1975

Figure 35
Mrs Kelley and Mr Kelley

- 76, when it would appear that a Mrs Judy A. Wilson took over as postmistress to deal with the ever increasing demand for Rattlesnake Island stamps. Little is known about Mrs Wilson other than she held the position of postmistress until the island was again sold in 1978 to John Adam, president of Tempcraft Inc., for the sum of $594,000. John Adam is said to have made the biggest improvements to the island with the restoration of the older buildings and the addition of a golf course. At the time John Adam acquired the island, Mrs Theresa M. Stewart (see Figure 40) was appointed as the fourth postmistress. Again there is a question mark as to how long she served, or if someone else took up the duty in the interim, prior to a lady

Figure 40
Theresa M. Stewart

by the name of Peggy Amey who apparently continued in the capacity of postmistress even though the issue of local post stamps of Rattlesnake Island ceased after the 1989 Owl set.

From 1966 to 1977 however, another notable figure, Virgil Fritz, served as postmaster at Port Clinton and had a close association with the island and its stamps, and was influential in son Bob's early and current interest in Rattlesnake Island stamps. Figures 36 and 37 show Virgil looking on as postal clerk Robert Lindemann prepares some of the 12,000 pieces of mail received for first day of issue cancelling, whilst the second picture shows him watching postal clerk Bernie Tibbs cancel more covers as Dr James P Frackelton looks on. Figure 38 shows historian, Bob Fritz.

Figure 36

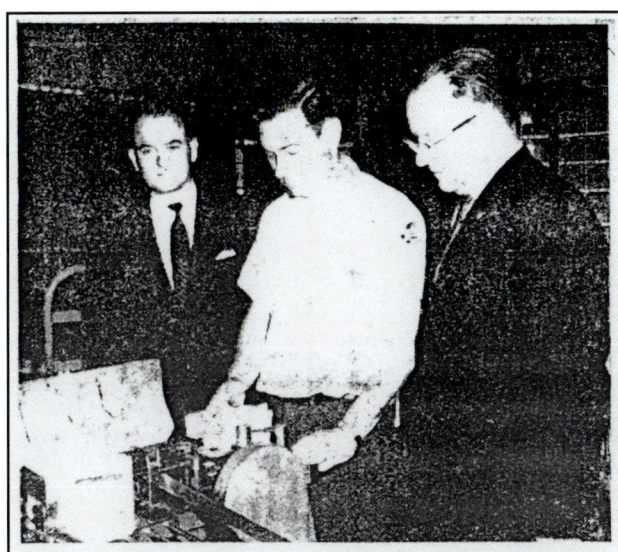

Bernie Tibbs, center, runs 12,000 pieces of mail through a cancellation machine Monday afternoon, all designated for nearly every part of the world, as first cancellation of the new triangle Rattlesnake Island stamps was made here. Looking on at left is James P. Frackelton, Westlake, O., president of the Rattlesnake Island Club. At right is Postmaster Virgil Fritz. First issue of the stamps were for stamp collectors.

Figure 37

Figure 38 Historian Bob Fritz

Another interesting story relates to a visit to Rattlesnake Island, whilst still owned by John Adam, by the famous entertainer Liza Minnelli. She is said to have stayed in the North Lodge and loved it so much that she asked to take the blueprints with her so that she could have a lodge built. There seems to be some doubt as to whether the drawings were ever returned. Adam sold the island and the established Rattlesnake Island Club to Lucius B. McKelvey and RI Resort Properties Inc., where the island became an exclusive club and where the cost of membership was almost $10,000 plus monthly fees. In fact the club was so exclusive that who the members were was a secret, even to other members.

In 1998, McKelvey put the island up for sale by auction, but the auction never transpired as it was bought by a consortium of some 65 members including Dr Frackelton, for around $5m. Plans were drawn up to resume issuing stamps in the early 1990s but failed to materialise. However, in a recent conversation between Dr Frackelton and the writer, stamps from Rattlesnake Island may yet make an appearance in the future, and if so, will I am sure, be greatly sought after. The island meantime, is privately owned and managed by The Rattlesnake island Club and is not open to the general public.

At present Griffing Airlines provides the only public transport to the island, flying to and from Sandusky, Ohio. With the demise of the local post, unmarked mail is carried by the airline to Sandusky where it is postmarked and fed into the main U.S. mailstream.

Recent information suggests that a new house has been built on the island complete with a helicopter pad. See Figure 39. Perhaps this will be the future mode of transport to and from the island and mean the demise of one or both of the runways and the land developed.

*Figure 39
Recent New Building and Helicopter Pad.*

NOTE:

The author would welcome any additional information about the stamps, covers, people, past and present, associated with the island, the Ford Tri-motor, early history of the island, present day mailing methods, in fact anything at all that may enhance or establish a more comprehensive record and useful reference for collectors of the future.

7. Catalogue of Stamp Issues

RATTLESNAKE ISLAND
LOCAL AIRMAIL POST 1966 - 1989
CATALOGUE OF STAMPS

Stamps printed by: Mueller Printing Company of Cleveland, Ohio - 1966 to 1972 issues.
Great Lakes Lithography Co., Cleveland, Ohio - 1973 to 1989 issues.
Each set of stamps were issued perforated and imperforate.
All perforated stamps - Perf'd 11¾
1966 stamps rectangular, all other printings are triangular.

Introductory Notes:

1. The first set of three stamps - 5c, 10c and 25c appeared in light somewhat pale washed out colours, but were re-printed in bolder darker colours. Of the three stamps, the 10c and 25c printings are easily distinguishable, the 5c is a little more difficult, but the map design in the first printing is a lighter shade of grey, whilst the second printing is darker with the islands more sharply defined and blacker in colour. The rectangular stamps were used only from 27th August to 9th December 1966.

2. No local post stamps were permitted to be adhered to mail from Rattlesnake Island to Port Clinton between 9th December 1966 and 22nd January 1967. During this period the use of rectangular stamps was prohibited by the United States Post Office but approval was subsequently given for triangular stamps to be used.

3. A number of perforation and colour error varieties are listed in this catalogue, but there is some doubt as to whether the perforation errors are genuine since the stamps were die-perforated, which means that it is virtually impossible for an

imperforate pair or block to appear in a perforated sheet. Spurious perforation errors could be created from imperforate sheets and collectors should be aware of possible unscrupulous vendors of such items.

4. Prices quoted in this catalogue are estimated prices one could expect to pay for mint never hinged stamps, based on information received and personal experience. Errors and covers, shown for collectors' interest, are also estimated prices as these can vary considerably in the philatelic market according to supply and demand, bearing in mind the increasing popularity of the Island's stamps and the limited amount of material available.

1966 - Features of Rattlesnake Island. (First Printing)
1st issue - rectangular shaped stamps.
First Day of Issue - 27th August 1966.
Printed in sheets of 20 without plate numbers.
Designer: James P. Frackelton, M.D.

PERFORATED
RS 1 - 5c Map of Rattlesnake Island
Colour: black and light grey with red text
Var. - 1 imperf. horizontally (pair)	US$30.00	UK£20.50
Var. - 2 imperf. at top	US$10.00	UK£ 6.75

RS 2 - 10c Ford Tri-motor approaching Island
Colour: pale green with black text
Var. - 1 black text shift to right	US$15.00	UK£10.25
Var. - 2 imperf. at top	US$12.50	UK£ 8.50
Var. - 3 imperf. at right	US$12.50	UK£ 8.50

RS 3 - 25c Boat and Dock
Colour: pale blue with black text
Var. - 1 red text	US$10.00	UK£ 6.75
Var. - 2 imperf. horizontally	US$20.00	UK£13.50
Var. - 3 imperf. at right	US$20.00	UK£13.50
Var. - 4 double perf. at left	US$15.00	UK£10.25
Var. - 5 imperf. at bottom	US$20.00	UK£13.50
Set of 3 - RS 1 - 3	**US$18.00**	**UK£13.00**

IMPERFORATE
RS 4 - 5c Map of Rattlesnake Island
Var. - 1 red text inverted	US$10.00	UK£ 6.75

RS 5 - 10c Ford Tri-motor approaching Island
Var. - 1 black text shift to right	US$15.00	UK£10.25

RS 6 - 25c Boat and Dock
Set of 3 - RS 4 - 6	**US$25.00**	**UK£18.25**

1966 - Features of Rattlesnake Island. (Second Printing)
1st issue - re-printed - rectangular shaped stamps.
Printed in sheets of 20 without plate numbers.
Designer: James P. Frackelton, M.D.

PERFORATED
RS 7 - 5c Map of Rattlesnake Island
Colour: black and grey with red text
Var. - 1 double perf. at right	US$12.50	UK£ 8.50
Var. - 2 double perf. into design (pair)	US$20.00	UK£13.50

RS 8 - 10c Ford Tri-motor approaching Island
Colour: green with black text
Var. - 1 double perf. at right	US$12.50	UK£ 8.50
Var. - 2 imperf. vertically	US$20.00	UK£13.50

RS 9 - 25c Boat and Dock
Colour: Blue with black text
Var. - 1 printed in green with black text	US$45.00	UK£30.50
Var. - 2 printed in green with black text (complete sheet)	US$550	UK£375
Var. - 3 double perf. at right	US$12.50	UK£ 8.50
Set of 3 - RS 7 - 9	**US$10.00**	**UK£7.25**

IMPERFORATE
RS 10 - 5c Map of Rattlesnake Island
RS 11 - 10c Ford Tri-motor approaching Island
Var. - 1 printed on both sides	US$50.00	UK£35.00

RS 12 - 25c Boat and Dock
Set of 3 - RS 10 -12	**US$12.00**	**UK£8.75**
No First Day Covers exist, earliest known cover - Sept. 22nd 1966	US$30.00	UK£20.00
Stampless Interim Cover	US$100	UK£68.00

NOTE: 9th December 1966 - 22nd January 1967
During this period when the use of rectangular Rattlesnake Island stamps was banned, and until approval had been given for triangular stamps to be used, mail continued to be processed with stampless covers which bore the large diamond cancel and a "fee paid" hand written in the lower left hand corner of the envelope. On 30th December 1966 stampless envelopes containing letters advising of the forthcoming issue of triangular stamps on 23rd January 1967, were sent to known regular collectors. Less than two hundred are believed to still exist.

1967 - Features of Rattlesnake Island. (Same Subjects as 1966)

2nd issue - triangular shaped stamps.
First Day of Issue - 23rd January 1967.
Printed in sheets of 20 with plate numbers.
Designer: James P. Frackelton, M.D.

PERFORATED
RS 13 - 5c Map of Rattlesnake Island
Colour: grey and black with red text
RS 14 - 10c Ford Tri-motor approaching Island
Colour: green with black text
RS 15 - 25c Boat and Dock
Colour: blue with black text
Set of 3 - RS 13 - 15	**US$6.00**	**UK£4.50**

IMPERFORATE
RS 16 - 5c Map of Rattlesnake Island
RS 17 - 10c Ford Tri-motor approaching Island
Var. - 1 black printing only	US$53.00	UK£35.85

RS 18 - 25c Boat and Dock
Var. - 1 double print	US$70.00	UK£47.50
Var. - 2 double print, one inverted	US$150	UK£100
Set of 3 - RS 16 - 18	**US$7.00**	**UK£5.25**

First Day Cover	Perf'd	US$5.50	UK£3.75
First Day Cover	Imperf	US$10.00	UK£6.75

Plate Numbers: With small Tri-motor motif and RILP.

5c	7 red;	8 black;
10c	9 green;	10 black;
25c	11 blue;	12 black

1968 - Birds and Sheep
3rd issue - triangular shaped stamps.
First Day of Issue - 22nd July 1968.
Printed in sheets of 20 with plate numbers and Ford Tri-motor in margins.
Designer: James P. Frackelton, M.D.

PERFORATED
RS 19 - 5c Gulls and Pier
Colour: multicoloured with magenta text
RS 20 - 10c Reeves Pheasant
Colour: multicoloured with black text
RS 21 - 25c Aoudads - North African Sheep
Colour: multicoloured with blue text

Set of 3 - RS 19 - 21	**US$5.00**	**UK£3.75**

IMPERFORATE
RS 22 - 5c Gulls and Pier

Var. - 1 blue colour missing	US$22.50	UK£15.25
Var. - 2 red and blue colours missing	US$22.50	UK£15.25
Var. - 3 blue and black colours missing	US$22.50	UK£15.25

RS 23 - 10c Reeves Pheasant

Var. - 1 blue colour missing	US$22.50	UK£15.25
Var. - 2 red and blue colours missing	US$22.50	UK£15.25
Var. - 3 blue and black colours missing	US$22.50	UK£15.25

RS 24 - 25c Aoudads - North African Sheep

Var. - 1 blue colour missing	US$22.50	UK£15.25
Var. - 2 red and blue colours missing	US$22.50	UK£15.25
Var. - 3 blue and black colours missing	US$22.50	UK£15.25
Set of 3 - RS 22 - 24	**US$6.00**	**UK£4.50**

First Day Cover	Perf'd	US$5.50	UK£3.75
First Day Cover	Imperf	US$10.00	UK£6.75

Plate Numbers: With small Tri-motor motif and RILP.

5c	13 yellow;	14 red;	15 blue;	16 black;
10c	17 yellow;	18 red;	19 blue;	20 black;
25c	21 yellow;	22 red;	23 blue;	24 black;

1969 - Sailing and Sunset
4th issue - triangular shaped stamps.
First Day of Issue - 1st December 1969.
Printed in sheets of 20 with plate numbers and Ford Tri-motor in margins.
Designer: James P. Frackelton, M.D.

PERFORATED
RS 25 - 5c Sailing Race
Colour: multicoloured with black text
Var. - 1 red colour missing
(price for a full sheet)   US$150   UK£100
Var. - 2 imperf. between   US$15.00   UK£10.25
RS 26 - 10c Lake Schooner
Colour: multicoloured with black text
Var. - 1 imperf. between   US$18.75   UK£12.75
RS 27 - 25c Island Sunset
Colour: multicoloured with black text
Var. - 1 imperf. between   US$21.00   UK£14.25
Set of 3 - RS 25 - 27   **US$5.00**   **UK£3.75**
IMPERFORATE
RS 28 - 5c Sailing Race
Var. - 1 blue colour missing   US$22.50   UK£15.20
RS 29 - 10c Lake Schooner
Var. - 1 blue colour missing   US$22.50   UK£15.20
RS 30 - 25c Island Sunset
Var. - 1 blue colour missing   US$22.50   UK£15.20
Set of 3 - RS 28 - 30   **US$6.00**   **UK£4.50**
First Day Cover   Perf'd   US$5.50   UK£3.75
First Day Cover   Imperf   US$10.00   UK£6.75

Plate Numbers: With small Tri-motor motif and RILP.
    5c   25 yellow;   26 red;   27 blue;   28 black;
    10c 29 yellow;   30 red;   31 blue;   32 black;
    25c 33 yellow;   34 red;   35 blue;   36 black;

1970 - Flowers

5th issue - triangular shaped stamps.
First Day of Issue - 2nd November 1970.
Printed in sheets of 20 with plate numbers and Ford Tri-motor in margins.
Designer: James P. Frackelton, M.D.

PERFORATED
RS 31 - 5c Pine Cone
Colour: multicoloured with black text
RS 32 - 10c Purple Scilla Hispanica
Colour: multicoloured with black text
RS 33 - 25c Red Columbine
Colour: multicoloured with black text
Set of 3 - RS 31 - 33   US$4.00   UK£3.00
IMPERFORATE
RS 34 - 5c Pine Cone
RS 35 - 10c Purple Scilla Hispanica
RS 36 - 25c Red Columbine
Set of 3 - RS 34 - 36   US$5.00   UK£3.75

First Day Cover   Perf'd   US$5.50   UK£3.75
First Day Cover   Imperf   US$10.00   UK£6.75

Plate Numbers: With small Tri-motor motif and RILP.

5c	37 yellow;	38 red;	39 blue;	40 black;
10c	41 yellow;	42 red;	43 blue;	44 black;
25c	45 yellow;	46 red;	47 blue;	48 black;

1971 - Rattlesnake Island Scenes
6th issue - triangular shaped stamps.
First Day of Issue - 23rd November 1971.
Printed in sheets of 20 with plate numbers and Ford Tri-motor in margins.
Designer: James P. Frackelton, M.D.

PERFORATED
RS 37 - 5c Gulls in Flight
Colour: multicoloured with black text
RS 38 - 10c Island Harbour
Colour: multicoloured with black text
Var. - 1 imperf. between   US$22.50   UK£15.20
RS 39 - 25c Main Lodge
Colour: multicoloured with black text
Var. - 1 imperf. between   US$22.50   UK£15.20
Set of 3 - RS 37 - 39   **US$4.00**   **UK£3.00**
IMPERFORATE
RS 40 - 5c Gulls in Flight
RS 41 - 10c Island Harbour
RS 42 - 25c Main Lodge
Set of 3 - RS 40 - 42   **US$5.00**   **UK£3.75**

First Day Cover   Perf'd   US$5.50   UK£3.75
First Day Cover   Imperf   US$10.00   UK£6.75

Plate Numbers: With small Tri-motor motif and RILP.
5c	49 yellow;	50 red;	51 blue;	52 black;
10c	53 yellow;	54 red;	55 blue;	56 black;
25c	57 yellow;	58 red;	59 blue;	60 black;

1972 - Sports and Sightseeing

7th Issue - triangular shaped stamps.
First Day of Issue - 16th November 1972.
Printed in sheets of 20 with plate numbers and Ford Tri-motor in margins.
Designer: James P. Frackelton, M.D.

PERFORATED
RS 43 - 5c Two Ladies Fishing
Colour: multicoloured with black text
RS 44 - 10c Island Tennis Court
Colour: multicoloured with black text
RS 45 - 25c Perry's Monument at Put-In-Bay
Colour: multicoloured with black text
(Perry's Monument)
RS 46 - 25c Perry's Monument at Put-In-Bay
Colour: multicoloured with black text
(Sightseeing)
Set of 4 - RS 43 - 46   US$7.00   UK£5.25
IMPERFORATE
RS 47 - 5c Two Ladies Fishing
RS 48 - 10c Island Tennis Court
RS 49 - 25c Perry's Monument at Put-In-Bay
RS 50 - 25c Perry's Monument at Put-In-Bay
Set of 4 - RS 47 - 50   US$8.00   UK£5.95

First Day Cover   Perf'd   US$5.50   UK£3.75
First Day Cover   Imperf   US$10.00   UK£6.75

Plate Numbers: With small Tri-motor motif and RILP.
　　　5c   61 yellow;   62 red;   63 blue;   64 black;
　　　10c   65 yellow;   66 red;   67 blue;   68 black;
　　　25c   69 yellow;   70 red;   71 blue;   72 black;

NOTE:
The two perforated stamps RS 45 - 'Perry's Monument' and RS 46 - 'Sightseeing' are from the same sheet with the wording alternating across the sheet. The same applies to the imperforate stamps RS 49 and RS 50

1973 - Lake Erie Fish
8th issue - triangular shaped stamps.
First Day of Issue - 13th November 1973.
Printed in sheets of 20 with plate numbers and Ford Tri-motor in margins.
Designer: Bernice Kochan.

PERFORATED
RS 51 - 5c Silver Catfish
Colour: multicoloured with black text
Var. - 1 black colour missing   US$22.50   UK£15.25
RS 52 - 10c Smallmouth Bass
Colour: multicoloured with black text
RS 53 - 25c Walleye
Colour: multicoloured with black text
Set of 3 - RS 51 - 53   **US$4.50**   **UK£3.25**
IMPERFORATE
RS 54 - 5c Silver Catfish
RS 55 - 10c Smallmouth Bass
RS 56 - 25c Walleye
Set of 3 - RS 54 - 56   **US$5.50**   **UK£4.00**

First Day Cover   Perf'd   US$5.50   UK£3.75
First Day Cover   Imperf   US$10.00   UK£6.75

Plate Numbers: With small Tri-motor motif and RILP.
    5c   70 yellow;   71 red;   72 blue;   73 black;
    10c   70 yellow;   71 red;   72 blue;   73 black;
    25c   70 yellow;   71 red;   72 blue;   73 black;

1974 - Native Birds *(First Postal Rate Increase)*
9th issue - triangular shaped stamps.
First Day of Issue - 19th November 1974.
Printed in sheets of 20 with plate numbers and Ford Tri-motor in margins.
Designer: Bernice Kochan.

PERFORATED
RS 57 - 20c Blue Jay
Colour: multicoloured with black text
RS 58 - 30c Bluebird
Colour: multicoloured with black text
RS 59 - 50c Red-Headed Woodpecker
Colour: multicoloured with black text
Set of 3 - RS 57 - 59   US$4.50   UK£3.25
IMPERFORATE
RS 60 - 20c Blue Jay
RS 61 - 30c Bluebird
RS 62 - 50c Red-Headed Woodpecker
Set of 3 - RS 60 - 62   US$5.50   UK£4.00

First Day Cover   Perf'd   US$5.50   UK£3.75
First Day Cover   Imperf   US$10.00   UK£6.75

Plate Numbers: With small Tri-motor motif and RILP.

20c	71 yellow;	72 red;	73 blue;	74 black;
30c	71 yellow;	72 red;	73 blue;	74 black;
50c	71 yellow;	72 red;	73 blue;	74 black;

1975 - Native Butterflies
10th issue - triangular shaped stamps.
First Day of Issue - 18th November 1975.
Printed in sheets of 20 with plate numbers and Ford Tri-motor in margins.
Designer: Bernice Kochan.

PERFORATED
RS 63 - 20c Clouded Sulphur
Colour: multicoloured with black text
RS 64 - 30c Black Swallowtail
Colour: multicoloured with black text
RS 65 - 50c Monarch
Colour: multicoloured with black text
Set of 3 - RS 63 - 65   US$4.50   UK£3.25
IMPERFORATE
RS 66 - 20c Clouded Sulphur
RS 67 - 30c Black Swallowtail
RS 68 - 50c Monarch
Set of 3 - RS 66 - 68   US$5.50   UK£4.00

First Day Cover   Perf'd   US$5.50   UK£3.75
First Day Cover   Imperf   US$10.00   UK£6.75

Plate Numbers: With small Tri-motor motif and RILP.
20c   72 yellow;   73 red;   74 blue;   75 black;
30c   72 yellow;   73 red;   74 blue;   75 black;
50c   72 yellow;   73 red;   74 blue;   75 black;

1976 - Flags, Celebrating U.S. Bicentennial & RI 10th Anniversary

11th issue - triangular shaped stamps.
First Day of Issue - 16th November 1976.
Printed in sheets of 20 with plate numbers and Ford Tri-motor in margins.
Designer: Bernice Kochan.

PERFORATED
RS 69 - 20c Don't Tread On Me
Colour: multicoloured with black text
RS 70 - 30c 13 Star United States Flag
Colour: multicoloured with black text
RS 71 - 50c 50 Star United States Flag
Colour: multicoloured with black text
Set of 3 - RS 69 - 71   US$4.50   UK£3.25
IMPERFORATE
RS 72 - 20c Don't Tread On Me
RS 73 - 30c 13 Star United States Flag
RS 74 - 50c 50 Star United States Flag
Set of 3 - RS 72 - 74   US$5.50   UK£4.00

First Day Cover   Perf'd   US$5.50   UK£3.75
First Day Cover   Imperf   US$10.00   UK£6.75

Plate Numbers: With small Tri-motor motif and RILP.
  20c   73 yellow;   74 red;   75 blue;   76 black;
  30c   73 yellow;   74 red;   75 blue;   76 black;
  50c   73 yellow;   74 red;   75 blue;   76 black;

1977 - Birds That Visit Rattlesnake Island
12th issue - triangular shaped stamps.
First Day of Issue - 15th November 1977.
Printed in sheets of 20 with plate numbers and Ford Tri-motor in margins.
Designer: Bernice Kochan.

PERFORATED
RS 75 - 20c Goldfinch (Wild Canary)
Colour: multicoloured with black text
RS 76 - 30c Indigo Bunting
Colour: multicoloured with black text
RS 77 - 50c Cardinal
Colour: multicoloured with black text
Set of 3 - RS 75 - 77   US$4.50   UK£3.25
IMPERFORATE
RS 78 - 20c Goldfinch (Wild Canary)
RS 79 - 30c Indigo Bunting
RS 80 - 50c Cardinal
Set of 3 - RS 78 - 80   US$5.50   UK£4.00

First Day Cover   Perf'd   US$5.50   UK£3.75
First Day Cover   Imperf   US$10.00   UK£6.75

Plate Numbers: With small Tri-motor motif and RILP.
    20c   74 yellow;   75 red;   76 blue;   77 black;
    30c   74 yellow;   75 red;   76 blue;   77 black;
    50c   74 yellow;   75 red;   76 blue;   77 black;

NOTE:
First Day Covers of this issue exist claiming to have been flown by Ford Tri-motor. The last remaining Tri-motor crashed in July 1977 and was not restored and returned into service until the Spring of 1980. Therefore, FDCs must have been conveyed by another type of aircraft.

1978 - Battleships of Lake Erie *(Second Postal Rate Increase)*
13th issue - triangular shaped stamps.
First Day of Issue - 22nd November 1978.
Printed in sheets of 20 with plate numbers and Ford Tri-motor in margins.
Designer: Trisha Marcum.

PERFORATED
RS 81 - 50c Sailing Vessel "Ariel"
Colour: multicoloured with black text
RS 82 - $1.00 Sailing Vessel "Detroit"
Colour: multicoloured with black text
RS 83 - $1.50 Sailing Vessel "Niagara"
Colour: multicoloured with black text
Set of 3 - RS 81 - 83   US$7.00   UK£5.25
IMPERFORATE
RS 84 - 50c Sailing Vessel "Ariel"
RS 85 - $1.00 Sailing Vessel "Detroit"
RS 86 - $1.50 Sailing Vessel "Niagara"
Set of 3 - RS 84 - 86   US$8.50   UK£6.25

First Day Cover   Perf'd   US$5.50   UK£3.75
First Day Cover   Imperf   US$10.00   UK£6.75

Plate Numbers: With small Tri-motor motif and RILP.
	76 yellow;	77 red;	78 blue;	79 black;
50c	76 yellow;	77 red;	78 blue;	79 black;
$1.00	76 yellow;	77 red;	78 blue;	79 black;
$1.50	76 yellow;	77 red;	78 blue;	79 black;

NOTE:
Unlike other issues, the year of issue date and the wording "Local Post" are missing from this set of warship designs depicting on the 50c stamp, the 100 ton sloop 'Ariel' with four guns, built June 1813, Presque Isle, Pennsylvania. The $1.00 stamp portrays the British Brig 'Detroit' of 490 tons built in 1813 with 19 guns, captured by Oliver Hazard Perry on September 10th 1813, whilst the $1.50 stamp shows the U. S. Brig of 480 tons also built at Presque Isle, Pennsylvania, with 20 guns. The remains of this ship were recovered from Misery Bay off Presque Isle in 1913 and rebuilt.

This set of stamps effectively commemorates the 165th Anniversary of the Battle of Lake Erie fought near Rattlesnake Island.

1979 - Wild Animals
14th issue - triangular shaped stamps.
First Day of Issue - 15th November 1979.
Printed in sheets of 20 with plate numbers and Ford Tri-motor in margins.
Designer: Robert Eisenbarth.

PERFORATED
RS 87 - 50c Chipmunk
Colour: multicoloured with black text
RS 88 - $1.00 Raccoon
Colour: multicoloured with black text
RS 89 - $1.50 Woodchuck
Colour: multicoloured with black text

Set of 3 - RS 87 - 89	**US$7.00**	**UK£5.25**

IMPERFORATE
RS 90 - 50c Chipmunk
RS 91 - $1.00 Raccoon
RS 92 - $1.50 Woodchuck

Set of 3 - RS 90 - 92	**US$8.50**	**UK£6.25**
First Day Cover Perf'd	US$15.00	UK£10.25
First Day Cover Imperf	US$17.50	UK£11.85

Plate Numbers: With small Tri-motor motif and RILP.

50c	77 yellow;	78 red;	79 blue;	80 black;
$1.00	77 yellow;	78 red;	79 blue;	80 black;
$1.50	77 yellow;	78 red;	79 blue;	80 black;

1980 - Insects

15th issue - triangular shaped stamps.
First Day of Issue - 21st November 1980.
Printed in sheets of 20 with plate numbers and Ford Tri-motor in margins.
Designer: Robert Eisenbarth.

PERFORATED
RS 93 - 50c Ladybug
Colour: multicoloured with black text
RS 94 - $1.00 Praying Mantis
Colour: multicoloured with black text
RS 95 - $1.50 Honeybee
Colour: multicoloured with black text
Set of 3 - RS 93 - 95   **US$7.00**   **UK£5.25**
IMPERFORATE
RS 96 - 50c Ladybug
RS 97 - $1.00 Praying Mantis
RS 98 - $1.50 Honeybee
Set of 3 - RS 96 - 98   **US$8.50**   **UK£6.25**

First Day Cover   Perf'd   US$15.00   UK£10.25
First Day Cover   Imperf   US$17.50   UK£11.85

Plate Numbers: With small Tri-motor motif and RILP.

50c	78 yellow;	79 red;	80 blue;	81 black;
$1.00	78 yellow;	79 red;	80 blue;	81 black;
$1.50	78 yellow;	79 red;	80 blue;	81 black;

1981 - Indian Artifacts *(Third Rate Increase)*
16th issue - triangular shaped stamps.
First Day of Issue - 16th November 1981.
Printed in sheets of 20 with plate numbers and Ford Tri-motor in margins.
Designer: Robert Eisenbarth.

PERFORATED
RS 99 - $1.00 Stone Axe
Colour: multicoloured with black text
RS 100 - $1.50 Indian Dwelling
Colour: multicoloured with black text
RS 101 - $2.00 Erie Tribesman
Colour: multicoloured with black text
Set of 3 - RS 99 - 101   US$8.50   UK£6.25
IMPERFORATE
RS 102 - $1.00 Stone Axe
RS 103 - $1.50 Indian Dwelling
RS 104 - $2.00 Erie Tribesman
Set of 3 - RS 102 - 104   US$9.50   UK£7.00

First Day Cover   Perf'd   US$15.00   UK£10.25
First Day Cover   Imperf   US$17.50   UK£11.85

Plate Numbers: With small Tri-motor motif and RILP.
$1.00	79 yellow;	80 red;	81 blue;	82 black;
$1.50	79 yellow;	80 red;	81 blue;	82 black;
$2.00	79 yellow;	80 red;	81 blue;	82 black;

1982 - Ducks of Lake Erie

17th issue - triangular shaped stamps.
First Day of Issue - 19th November 1982.
Printed in sheets of 20 with plate numbers and Ford Tri-motor in margins.
Designer: Robert Eisenbarth.

PERFORATED
RS 105 - $1.00 Mallard
Colour: multicoloured with black text
RS 106 - $1.50 Hooded Merganser
Colour: multicoloured with black text
RS 107 - $2.00 Wood Duck
Colour: multicoloured with black text
Set of 3 - RS 105 - 107   US$8.50   UK£6.25
IMPERFORATE
RS 108 - $1.00 Mallard
RS 109 - $1.50 Hooded Merganser
RS 110 - $2.00 Wood Duck
Set of 3 - RS 108 - 110   US$9.50   UK£7.00

First Day Cover   Perf'd   US$15.00   UK£10.25
First Day Cover   Imperf   US$17.50   UK£11.85

Plate Numbers: With small Tri-motor motif and RILP.
  $1.00 80 yellow; 81 red; 82 blue; 83 black;
  $1.50 80 yellow; 81 red; 82 blue; 83 black;
  $2.00 80 yellow; 81 red; 82 blue; 83 black;

1983 - Rattlesnake Island Buildings

18th issue - triangular shaped stamps.
First Day of Issue - 18th November 1983.
Printed in sheets of 20 with plate numbers and Ford Tri-motor in margins.
Designer: Robert Eisenbarth.

PERFORATED
RS 111 - $1.00 Marina
Colour: multicoloured with black text
RS 112 - $1.50 Lighthouse
Colour: multicoloured with black text
RS 113 - $2.00 Recreation Centre
Colour: multicoloured with black text
Set of 3 - RS 111 - 113   US$8.50   UK£6.25
IMPERFORATE
RS 114 - $1.00 Marina
RS 115 - $1.50 Lighthouse
RS 116 - $2.00 Recreation Centre
Set of 3 - RS 114 - 116   US$9.50   UK£7.00

First Day Cover   Perf'd   US$15.00   UK£10.25
First Day Cover   Imperf   US$17.50   UK£11.85

Plate Numbers: With small Tri-motor motif and RILP.
   $1.00 81 yellow;   82 red;   83 blue;   84 black;
   $1.50 81 yellow;   82 red;   83 blue;   84 black;
   $2.00 81 yellow;   82 red;   83 blue;   84 black;

1984 - Wild Flowers
19th issue - triangular shaped stamps.
First Day of Issue - 19th November 1984.
Printed in sheets of 20 with plate numbers and Ford Tri-motor in margins.
Designer: Robert Eisenbarth.

PERFORATED
RS 117 - $1.00 Trout Lily
Colour: multicoloured with black text
RS 118 - $1.50 White Trillium
Colour: multicoloured with black text
RS 119 - $2.00 Wild Aster
Colour: multicoloured with black text
Set of 3 - RS 117 - 119   US$8.50   UK£6.25
IMPERFORATE
RS 120 - $1.00 Trout Lily
RS 121 - $1.50 White Trillium
RS 122 - $2.00 Wild Aster
Set of 3 - RS 120 - 122   US$9.50   UK£7.00

First Day Cover   Perf'd   US$15.00   UK£10.25
First Day Cover   Imperf   US$17.50   UK£11.85

Plate Numbers: With small Tri-motor motif and RILP.
$1.00   82 yellow;   83 red;   84 blue;   85 black;
$1.50   82 yellow;   83 red;   84 blue;   85 black;
$2.00   82 yellow;   83 red;   84 blue;   85 black;

1985 - Island Wildlife

20th issue - triangular shaped stamps.
First Day of Issue - 14th November 1985.
Printed in sheets of 20 with plate numbers and Ford Tri-motor in margins.
Designer: Robert Eisenbarth.

PERFORATED
RS 123 - $1.00 Fox Squirrel
Colour: multicoloured with black text
RS 124 - $1.50 White-Tailed Deer
Colour: multicoloured with black text
RS 125 - $2.00 Wild Turkey
Colour: multicoloured with black text
Set of 3 - RS 123 - 125   US$8.50   UK£6.25
IMPERFORATE
RS 126 - $1.00 Fox Squirrel
RS 127 - $1.50 White-Tailed Deer
RS 128 - $2.00 Wild Turkey
Set of 3 - RS 126 - 128   US$9.50   UK£7.00

First Day Cover   Perf'd   US$15.00   UK£10.25
First Day Cover   Imperf   US$17.50   UK£11.85

Plate Numbers: With small Tri-motor motif and RILP.

$1.00	83 yellow;	84 red;	85 blue;	86 black;
$1.50	83 yellow;	84 red;	85 blue;	86 black;
$2.00	83 yellow;	84 red;	85 blue;	86 black;

1986 - 20th Anniversary Single Design
21st issue - triangular shaped stamps.
First Day of Issue - 27th August 1986.
Printed in sheets of 20 with plate numbers and Ford Tri-motor in margins.
Designer: Robert Eisenbarth.

PERFORATED
**RS 129 - $2.00 Ford Tri-motor in flight
over Rattlesnake Island**   US$25.00   UK£16.75
Colour: multicoloured with black text
IMPERFORATE
**RS 130 - $2.00 Ford Tri-motor in flight
over Rattlesnake Island**   US$25.00   UK£16.75
Colour: multicoloured with black text
Commemorative Folder   US$75.00   UK£50.00

THE FORD TRIMOTOR, nicknamed the "Tin Goose," was designed by pioneer aircraft designer Bill Stout, and was one of the first coast-to-coast carriers of U.S. mail. Ford built 198 of the planes between 1928 and 1933, and it was one of these rugged craft that carried Adm. Richard Byrd on his historic flight over the South Pole in 1929. The "Tin Goose" cruised at only 85 mph, but carried heavy loads and could land on and take off from grassy strips and short runways, such as the 1,700-foot runway on Rattlesnake Island.

Rattlesnake Island, an 85-acre privately-owned resort, is located in western Lake Erie near Port Clinton, Ohio. It established its own postal service on Aug. 27, 1966, after requests to the U.S. Postal Department for mail service, beginning in 1959, were repeatedly denied. U.S. postal regulations allow areas not served by post offices to issue their own local stamps to convey mail to the nearest U.S. post office. Regular U.S. postage is required to carry the mail for further delivery.

Mail was carried between the island and Port Clinton in a Ford Trimotor airplane of Island Airlines, making Rattlesnake Island's the only airmail local post in the U.S. The airline's last Trimotor was grounded in 1980 after nearly 50 years' service, but the company — the world's shortest airline, with its longest flight only about six miles — continues to carry the island's mail in its more modern craft.

The island's first issue was a set of three rectangular stamps — 5 cents, black and red, showing a chart of the Lake Erie islands; 10 cents, green and black, aerial view of the island and a Ford Trimotor; and 25 cents, blue and black, harbor scene.

On Dec. 9 1966, however, the postal department issued an order to the Port Clinton post office that mail bearing the Rattlesnake Island local stamps could not enter the U.S. mails. The legality of the stamps was not questioned, but it was felt that the Rattlesnake Island stamps were too attractive and might be confused with U.S. postage. It was finally agreed that triangular stamps would be satisfactory since the U.S. has never used that format.

A new set of triangular stamps was issued on Jan. 23, 1967, with the same basic designs, colors and denominations as the original issue. The island's stamps have been triangular ever since and, beginning in 1968, have been printed in full color in sheets of 20, both perforated and imperforate, with plate numbers.

During the interval between the first two issues, the local post continued, using only the island's diamond-shaped cancel.

Three stamps have been issued each year since the local post's inception, with the lowest rate for post cards, the middle value for letters and the highest rate for parcels. Designs of all stamps are directly related to the island and its surrounding area, and have included island scenes and activities, wildlife and historical themes.

Mrs. Theresa M. Stewart has been postmistress for the island since 1979. Stamp designer since 1979 has been Robert Eisenbarth.

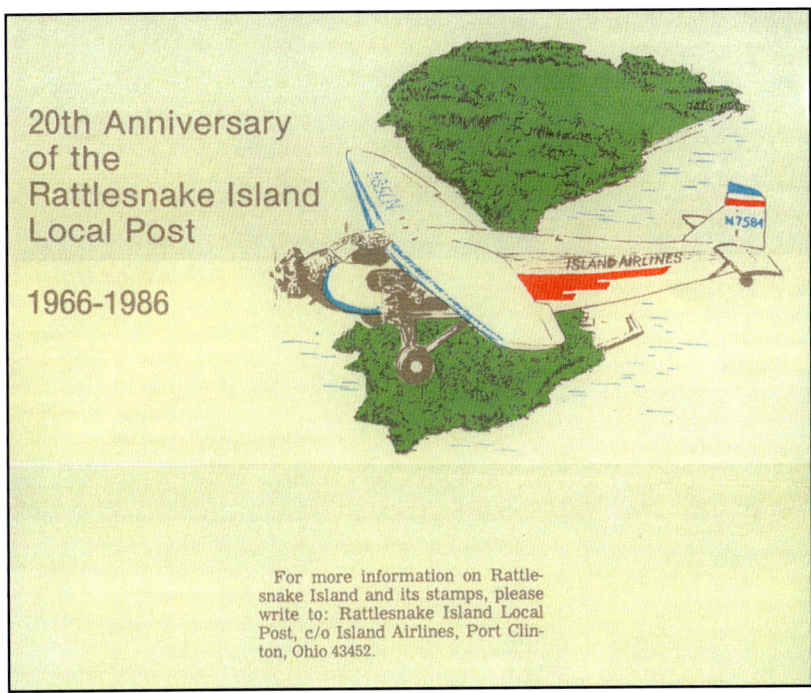

NOTE:
The 1986 20th Anniversary of Rattlesnake Island's Local Post was commemorated with a single stamp design perforated and imperforate, and issued as single stamps, in sheets, and in a special folder measuring $6^1/_2$" x $3^1/_2$" containing a postal card with either the perforate or imperforate stamp attached and cancelled 27th August 1986, with text at the side giving a short history of the local post. The original price for this item was $5.00.

1986 - Lake Erie Waterfowl
22nd issue - triangular shaped stamps.
First Day of Issue - 12th November 1986.
Printed in sheets of 20 with plate numbers and Ford Tri-motor in margins.
Designer: Robert Eisenbarth.

PERFORATED
RS 131 - $1.00 Canada Goose
Colour: multicoloured with black text
RS 132 - $1.50 Herring Gull
Colour: multicoloured with black text
RS 133 - $2.00 Great Blue Heron
Colour: multicoloured with black text
Set of 3 - RS 131 - 133   US$8.50   UK£6.25
IMPERFORATE
RS 134 - $1.00 Canada Goose
RS 135 - $1.50 Herring Gull
RS 136 - $2.00 Great Blue Heron
Set of 3 - RS 134 - 136   US$9.50   UK£7.00

First Day Cover   Perf'd   US$15.00   UK£10.25
First Day Cover   Imperf   US$17.50   UK£11.85

Plate Numbers: With small Tri-motor motif and RILP.
$1.00 84 yellow;   85 red;   86 blue;   87 black;
$1.50 84 yellow;   85 red;   86 blue;   87 black;
$2.00 84 yellow;   85 red;   86 blue;   87 black;

1987 - Lake Erie Watercraft

23rd issue - triangular shaped stamps.
First Day of Issue - 12th November 1987.
Printed in sheets of 20 with plate numbers and Ford Tri-motor in margins.
Designer: Robert Eisenbarth.

PERFORATED
RS 137 - $1.00 The Niagara
Colour: multicoloured with black text
RS 138 - $1.50 Ore Carrier
Colour: multicoloured with black text
RS 139 - $2.00 Pleasure Craft
Colour: multicoloured with black text
Set of 3 - RS 137 - 139   US$8.50   UK£6.25
IMPERFORATE
RS 140 - $1.00 The Niagara
RS 141 - $1.50 Ore Carrier
RS 142 - $2.00 Pleasure Craft
Set of 3 - RS 140 - 142   US$9.50   UK£7.00

First Day Cover   Perf'd   US$15.00   UK£10.25
First Day Cover   Imperf   US$17.50   UK£11.85

Plate Numbers: With small Tri-motor motif and RILP.
    $1.00 84 yellow;   85 red;   86 blue;   87 black;
    $1.50 84 yellow;   85 red;   86 blue;   87 black;
    $2.00 84 yellow;   85 red;   86 blue;   87 black;

1988 - Lighthouses
24th issue - triangular shaped stamps.
First Day of Issue - 12th November 1988.
Printed in sheets of 20 with plate numbers and Ford Tri-motor in margins.
Designer: Robert Eisenbarth.

PERFORATED
RS 143 - $1.00 Old Port Clinton, Ohio Lighthouse
Colour: multicoloured with black text
RS 144 - $1.50 Rattlesnake Island Lighthouse
Colour: multicoloured with black text
RS 145 - $2.00 Marblehead, Ohio Lighthouse
Colour: multicoloured with black text
Set of 3 - RS 143 - 145   US$8.50   UK£6.25
IMPERFORATE
RS 146 - $1.00 Old Port Clinton, Ohio Lighthouse
RS 147 - $1.50 Rattlesnake Island Lighthouse
RS 148 - $2.00 Marblehead, Ohio Lighthouse
Set of 3 - RS 146 - 148   US$9.50   UK£7.00

First Day Cover   Perf'd   US$15.00   UK£10.25
First Day Cover   Imperf   US$17.50   UK£11.85

Plate Numbers: With small Tri-motor motif and RILP.
$1.00 85 yellow;   86 red;   87 blue;   88 black;
$1.50 85 yellow;   86 red;   87 blue;   88 black;
$2.00 85 yellow;   86 red;   87 blue;   88 black;

1989 - Owls

25th issue - triangular shaped stamps.
First Day of Issue - 20th November 1989.
Printed in sheets of 20 with plate numbers and Ford Tri-motor in margins.
Designer: Robert Eisenbarth.

PERFORATED
RS 149 - $1.00 Barn Owl
Colour: multicoloured with black text
RS 150 - $1.50 Great Horned Owl
Colour: multicoloured with black text
RS 151 - $2.00 Snowy Owl
Colour: multicoloured with black text
Set of 3 - RS 149 - 151   US$8.50   UK£6.25
IMPERFORATE
RS 152 - $1.00 Barn Owl
RS 153 - $1.50 Great Horned Owl
RS 154 - $2.00 Snowy Owl
Set of 3 - RS 152 - 154   US$9.50   UK£7.00

First Day Cover   Perf'd   US$15.00   UK£10.25
First Day Cover   Imperf   US$17.50   UK£11.85

Plate Numbers: With small Tri-motor motif and RILP.
  $1.00 86 yellow;   87 red;   88 blue;   89 black;
  $1.50 86 yellow;   87 red;   88 blue;   89 black;
  $2.00 86 yellow;   87 red;   88 blue;   89 black;

NOTE:
The printing and issue of local post stamps was discontinued after the 1989 issue.

8. Rattlesnake Island Local Post Cancellations

Mail Cancellation Marks

Type 1.
Diamond shaped with inner frame line
53 x 35mm used on on mail 1966 - 1972.

Colours used. Year.

Violet	1966 - 1970, 1973 - 1974.
Blue	1966 - 1970, 1972.
Red	1969, 1971 - 1972, 1977.
Black	1966 - 1969, 1972 - 1973, 1976, 1978.
Blue-green	1966, 1968, 1972

Type 2.
Diamond shaped without inner frame line
53 x 35mm used on mail 1973 - 1989.

Colours used. Year

Violet	1973 - 1989.
Black	1973 - 1978.
Red	1976 - 1977.

9. Rattlesnake Island Local Post

Ford Tri-motor Markings

Type 1.
Rubberstamped Plane - 50 x 24mm used on mail 1967 - 1970 and 1972.

Colours used.   Red.   Reddish-Brown.

Type 2.
Rubberstamped Plane - 36 x 16mm used on mail 1968 - 1976, 1978.
Note: Small letters, wide "V" in "Via" "D" away from rudder.

Colours used. Red.   Black.   Violet.   Blue

Type 3.
Printed Plane - 36 x 17mm used on mail 1975 - 1989.
Note: Larger letters, narrow "V" in "Via" "D" close to rudder.

Colours used. Black.

Type 4.
Printed Plane - 35 x 18mm used on mail 1978.
Note: "Rattlesnake Island" centered above plane.

Colours used. Black.

10. Rattlesnake Island Local Post

Inscriptions

Type 1.
Rubberstamped single-line border rectangular panel embracing 4 lines of text.
Size: 65 x 23mm used on mail - 1967, 1969 and 1970.
Colours used:
Purple, Black, Blue, Red.

RATTLESNAKE ISLAND LOCAL POST
FORD TRI-MOTOR MAIL SERVICE BETWEEN
RATTLESNAKE ISLAND AND PORT CLINTON, OHIO
TRIANGULAR ISSUE FIRST DAY JAN. 23, 1967

Type 2.
Rubberstamped single-line border rectangular panel embracing 4 lines of text.
Size: 71 x 23mm used on mail - 1968.
Colours used:
Purple, Black, Blue, Red.

RATTLESNAKE ISLAND LOCAL POST
FORD TRI-MOTOR MAIL SERVICE BETWEEN
RATTLESNAKE ISLAND AND PORT CLINTON, OHIO
THIRD REGULAR ISSUE FIRST DAY JULY 22, 1968

Type 3.
Rubberstamped single-line border rectangular panel embracing 4 lines of text.
Size: 60 x 20mm used on mail - 1971 - 1974.
Colours used:
Purple, Blue, Red.

RATTLESNAKE ISLAND LOCAL POST
FORD TRI-MOTOR MAIL SERVICE BETWEEN
RATTLESNAKE ISLAND AND PORT CLINTON, OHIO
1972 ISSUE FIRST DAY NOV. 16, 1972

Type 4.
Printed single-line border rectangular panel embracing 4 lines of text.
Size: 62 x 20mm used on mail - 1975 - 1977.
Colours used:
Black.

RATTLESNAKE ISLAND LOCAL POST
FORD TRI-MOTOR MAIL SERVICE BETWEEN
RATTLESNAKE ISLAND AND PORT CLINTON, OHIO
12TH ISSUE FIRST DAY NOV. 15, 1977

Type 5.
Printed single-line border rectangular panel embracing 4 lines of text.
Size: 62 x 21mm used on mail - 1978, 1988 - 1989.
Colours used:
Black.

```
RATTLESNAKE ISLAND LOCAL POST
FORD TRI-MOTOR MAIL SERVICE BETWEEN
RATTLESNAKE ISLAND AND PORT CLINTON, OHIO
13TH. ISSUE FIRST DAY NOV. 22, 1978
```

Type 6. Printed single-line border rectangular panel embracing 4 lines of text.
Size: 72 x 21mm used on mail - 1979, 1987.
Colours used: Black.

    No examples to hand

Type 7. Printed single-line border rectangular panel embracing 3 lines of text.
Size: 60 x 16mm used on mail - 1978 - 1982, 1986.
Colours used: Black.

    No examples to hand

Type 8. Printed single-line border rectangular panel embracing 3 lines of text.
Size: 71 x 15mm used on mail - 1979, 1983 - 1984, 1986.
Colours used: Black.

```
RATTLESNAKE ISLAND LOCAL POST
FORD TRI-MOTOR MAIL SERVICE BETWEEN
RATTLESNAKE ISLAND AND PORT CLINTON, OHIO
```

Type 9. Printed single-line border rectangular panel embracing 2 lines of text.
    Size: 34 x 12mm used on mail - 1966 - 1967.
Colours used: Blue, Black, Violet, Red.

11. Known U.S. Post Office Cancellations on Rattlesnake Island

Local Post Covers

City	Years Used	Description
Caledonia	1976	Double ring hand cancel magenta
Cleveland	1978	Wavy line machine cancel with Zip Code
	1992	Spray marking
Port Clinton	1966	Wavy line machine cancel without Zip Code
	1966 - 1989	Wavy line machine cancel with Zip Code
	1970	Double ring hand cancel
	1981	Four bar hand cancel
	1984, 1986	Double ring hand cancel with wavy killer bars
	1988	Double ring hand cancel in magenta
Sandusky	1968	Wavy line machine cancel with Zip Code
	1976	Double ring hand cancel in magenta
Toledo	1979-80	Slogan machine cancel with Zip Code
	1983	Four bar hand cancel
USPS, OH	1975	Slogan machine cancel with Zip Code

12. A Selection of Stamp Errors - Genuine or...?

Normal   Error
1966 25c Colour Error

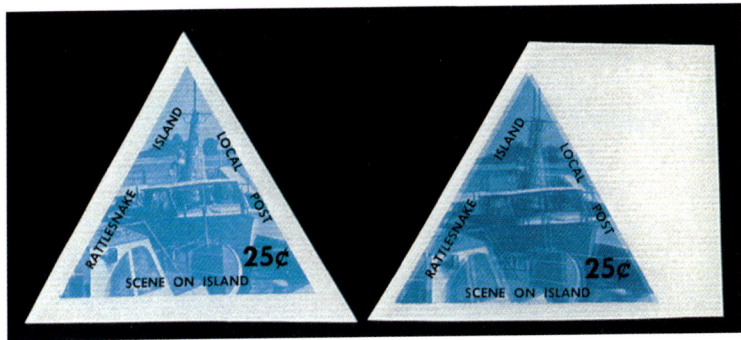

Normal   Error
1967 25c Imperf. Double Print

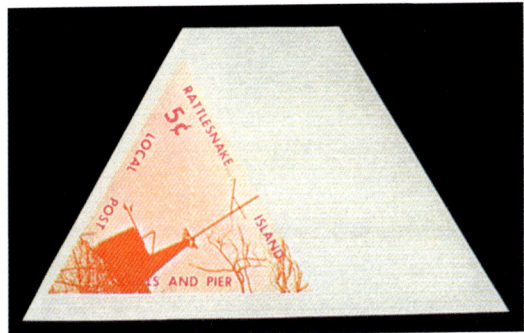

1968 5c Missing Colours

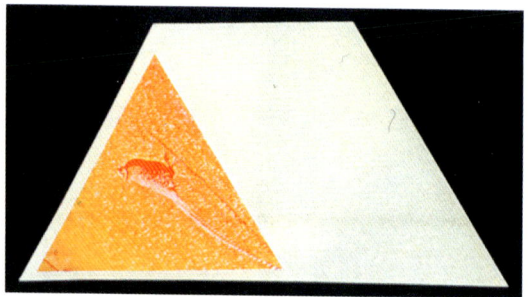

1968 10c Missing Colours & Missing Value

1968 25c Missing Colours

1966. 1st Printing 25c Dock - Imperforate Horizontally.

1966. 2nd Printing 5c Map - Imperforate Horizontally.

1966. 2nd Printing 25c Blue Dock - Green Colour Error.

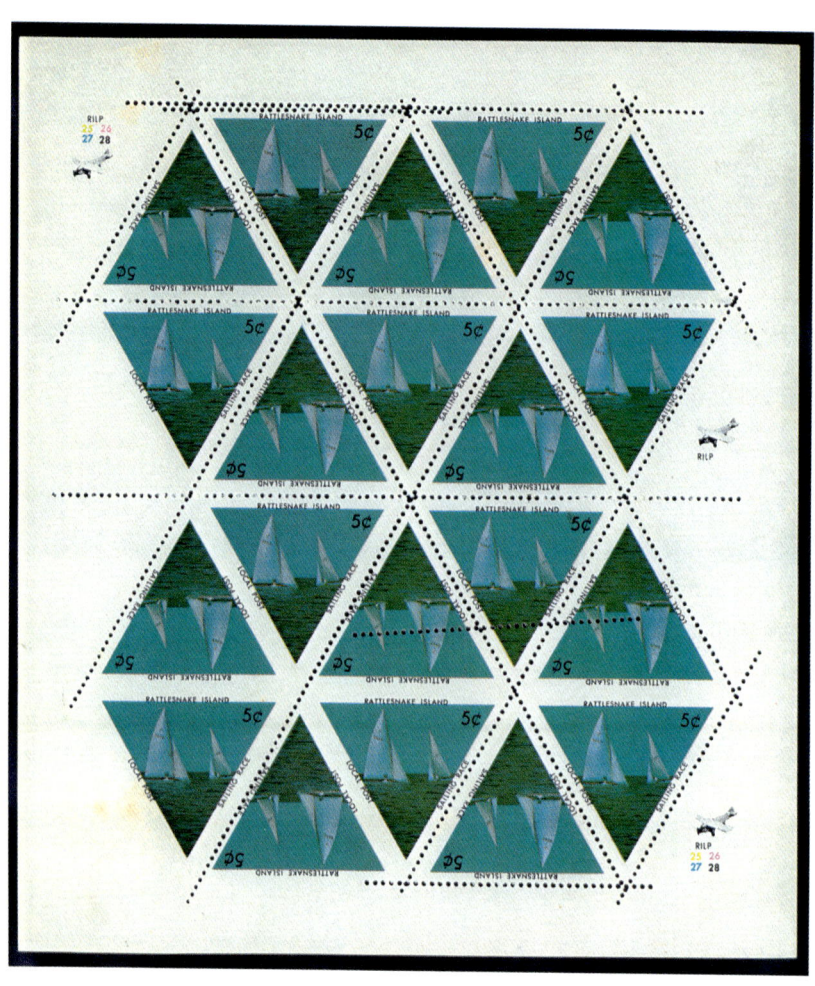

1969. Issue 5c Yachts - Perforation Error.

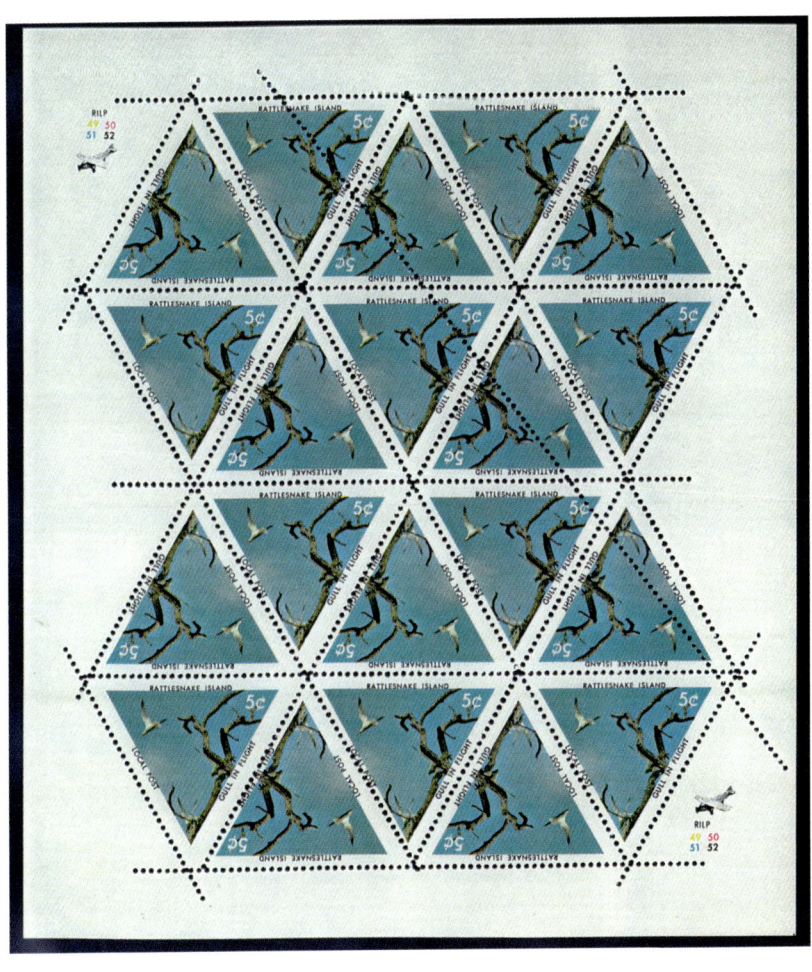

1971. Issue 5c Gulls In Flight - Perforation Error.

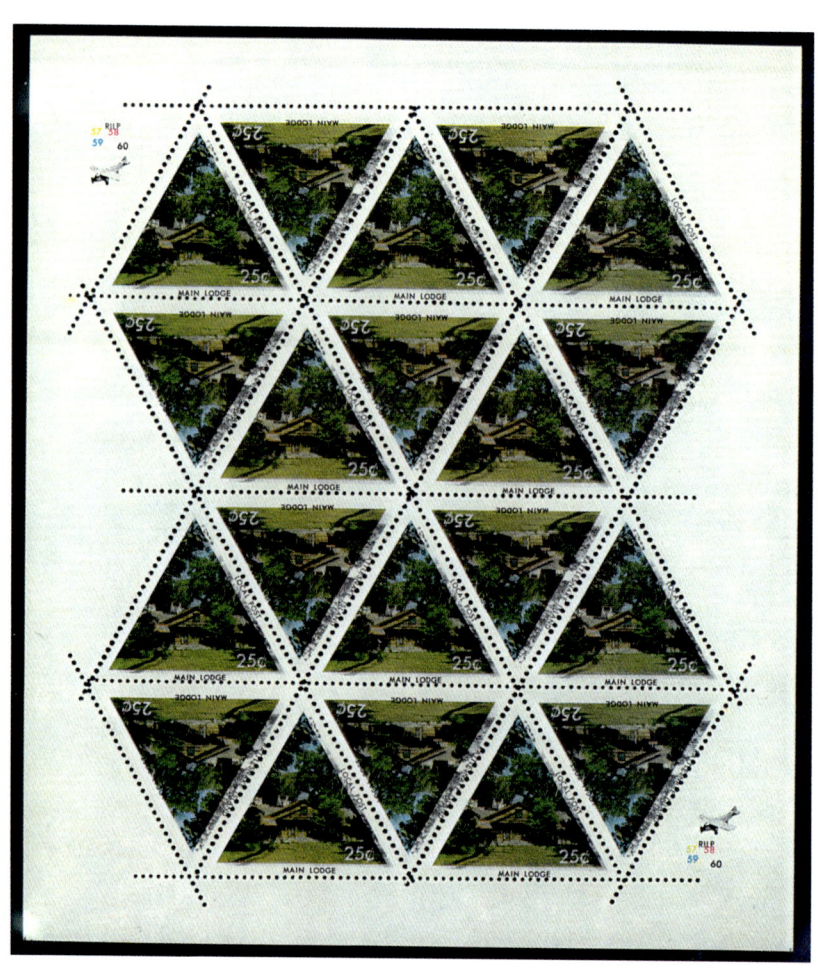

1971. Issue 25c Main Lodge - Print Shift Error.

STAMP ORDER FORM

Rattlesnake Island Local Post

1st ISSUE — RECTANGULAR — AUGUST 27, 1966
2nd ISSUE — TRIANGULAR — JANUARY 23, 1967
XXXX INDICATES NOT AVAILABLE

Rattlesnake Island Local Post

STAMP ORDER FORM

	1st ISSUE PERF.	1st ISSUE IMPERF.	2nd ISSUE PERF.	2nd ISSUE IMPERF.	TOTAL
SET OF 3 STAMPS AT 40c A SET 5c, 10c, 25c					
FIRST DAY OF ISSUE COVERS AT 50c PER COVER (set of 3 stamps)	XXXX XXXX	XXXX XXXX			
COMPLETE SHEET OF 5c STAMPS (Post Card Rate) 20 STAMPS @ $1.00					
COMPLETE SHEET OF 10c STAMPS (Letter Rate) 20 STAMPS @ $2.00					
COMPLETE SHEET OF 25c STAMPS (Parcel Post Rate) 20 STAMPS @ $5.00					
PLATE NO. BLOCKS OF 5c 6 STAMPS @ 30c	XXXX XXXX	XXXX XXXX			
PLATE NO. BLOCKS OF 10c 6 STAMPS @ 60c	XXXX XXXX	XXXX XXXX			
PLATE NO. BLOCKS OF 25c 6 STAMPS @ 1.50	XXXX XXXX	XXXX XXXX			
FLOWN COVERS AFTER 1st DAY OF ISSUE AT 50c PER COVER.		XXXX XXXX			
	First Issue Limited Stock Available		TOTAL		

PLEASE MAKE CHECKS OR MONEY ORDERS TO:

RATTLESNAKE ISLAND, INC.
RATTLESNAKE ISLAND, OHIO
c/o ISLAND AIRLINES
PORT CLINTON, OHIO 43452

NAME ______________________
STREET ______________________
CITY ______________________
STATE ______________ ZIP ________
PLEASE WRITE SPECIAL ORDERS ON BACK

Figure 41 First Stamp Issue - Order Form

Rattlesnake Island Local Post

1st ISSUE — RECTANGULAR — AUGUST 27, 1966
NO LONGER AVAILABLE

2nd ISSUE — TRIANGULAR — JANUARY 23, 1967
3rd ISSUE — ANIMALS & BIRDS — JULY 22, 1968

Rattlesnake Island Local Post

STAMP ORDER FORM

	3rd ISSUE PERF.	3rd ISSUE IMPERF.	2nd ISSUE PERF.	2nd ISSUE IMPERF.	TOTAL
SET OF 3 STAMPS AT 40c A SET 5c, 10c, 25c					
COMPLETE SHEET OF 5c STAMPS (Post Card Rate) 20 STAMPS @ $1.00					
COMPLETE SHEET OF 10c STAMPS (Letter Rate) 20 STAMPS @ $2.00					
COMPLETE SHEET OF 25c STAMPS (Parcel Post Rate) 20 STAMPS @ $5.00					
PLATE NO. BLOCKS OF 5c 6 STAMPS @ 30c					
PLATE NO. BLOCKS OF 10c 6 STAMPS @ 60c					
PLATE NO. BLOCKS OF 25c 6 STAMPS @ 1.50					
FLOWN COVERS AFTER 1st DAY OF ISSUE AT 50c PER COVER (set of 3 stamps)					
POST CARDS OF ISLAND OR FORD TRI-MOTOR AT 25c EACH (5c local & U.S. Stamp Inc.)					
FIRST ISSUE HAS NOT BEEN USED ON COVER SINCE DECEMBER 13, 1966 (No longer available)				TOTAL	

MINIMUM ORDER 50c PLEASE

PLEASE MAKE CHECKS OR MONEY ORDERS TO:

RATTLESNAKE ISLAND, INC.
RATTLESNAKE ISLAND, OHIO
c/o ISLAND AIRLINES
PORT CLINTON, OHIO 43452

NAME ______________________
STREET ______________________
CITY ______________________
STATE ______________ ZIP ________
PLEASE WRITE SPECIAL ORDERS ON BACK

Figure 42 First Triangular Stamp Issue - Order Form

Aerial views of Rattlesnake Island